CRICKET MAD

*

Michael Parkinson was born in a part of Yorkshire where it was perfectly normal to be cricket mad. Which is the reason he was not stared at as he ran to the shops in a perfect imitation of Fred Trueman's bowling approach or dived out of bus queues to catch Cyril Washbrook at first slip off Johnny Wardle. Since reaching a mature age and moving down south he has learned to curb his madness.

His wife too is cricket mad. The marriage has been blessed with three children: one fast bowler, one opening bat and a future captain of M.C.C. When he is not dreaming about cricket he writes about it in *The Sunday Times* and *Punch*.

He is not a member of the M.C.C. because he doesn't speak the language and moreover has an irresistible desire to take his shirt off whenever he goes to Lords.

His favourite ground is Bramall Lane, his favourite flower is a white rose and his favourite cricketers are Yorkshiremen. He is renowned throughout cricket for the detached and unbiased flavour of his writing.

Also in Arrow Books by Michael Parkinson
Football Daft

Michael Parkinson

Cricket Mad

drawings by
DEREK ALDER

ARROW BOOKS

ARROW BOOKS LTD
3 Fitzroy Square, London W1

AN IMPRINT OF THE HUTCHINSON GROUP

London Melbourne Sydney Auckland
Wellington Johannesburg Cape Town
and agencies throughout the world

First published by
Stanley Paul & Co. Ltd 1969
Arrow edition 1973

*Made and printed in Great Britain
by Hunt Barnard Printing Ltd,
Aylesbury, Bucks.*

ISBN 0 09 908140 7

Contents

BOOK 1 FORMATIVE YEARS

Some parts of this book have been developed from articles which I originally wrote for the *Sunday Times* and *Punch*, and I am grateful to the editors of both for allowing me to call on this material.

Michael Parkinson

BOOK 2 SECOND INNINGS

BOOK 1 Formative years

If a Sport's not worth fighting about
it's not worth playing

OLD YORKSHIRE SAYING

1 'What's bred in the bone'

When I was born my paternal grandmother tried very hard to have me called Melbourne because MCC had just won a test match there. Fortunately my mother, a southerner of great common sense, would have none of it. Not so my father who, being a Yorkshireman and therefore cricket mad, was torn between Herbert (Sutcliffe), Percy (Holmes) or Hedley (Verity). Mother, fortunately, settled for Michael and would not budge. That was the only concession my old man made during the next twenty years which he devoted to producing a son who would one day play for Yorkshire. His approach was entirely scientific. For instance much research on various cricket fields as a fast bowler of fearsome reputation had left him with a healthy respect for left-handed batsmen. That being so he turned me into a left-handed bat against my natural inclinations.

At eleven I was playing in the team he captained, a child among men, a pimple among muscles. But I received no quarter because the old man would not have it that way. That I survived that period intact, considering the atrocious wickets we played on and the psychotic bowlers we faced, was due to my own fleet footedness and not as my father used to insist to the rumour that God protected prospective Yorkshire cricketers. He based this on the fact that He was born just outside Barnsley.

After every game came the post mortem, the old man dissecting every innings I played, advising, criticising, stuffing my young head with the games folk lore. There was nothing selfish in this. He would have done the same for any kid my age because he couldn't stand the game being played badly. Only once did he use my tender years to his advantage. We were playing at a ground near Barnsley on a wicket which gave every impression of being prepared by a mechanical trench digger. We got our opponents out for about 40 and were in trouble at 24 for 7 when the old man joined me at the wicket. He came to me and said:

'Just keep your head down and leave the rest to me.'

He walked to the non-striker's end and immediately engaged in conversation with their fast bowler who had taken five wickets and put two of our players into the casualty ward. As the fast bowler walked back to his mark the old man walked with him.

'Long run for an off spinner,' he said as they walked side by side.

'Wheer's tha' think tha's going?' said the fast bowler, stopping on his walk back.

'Wi' thee,' said the old man.

'Ay up umpire,' said the bowler. 'Can't tha' stop him?'

The umpire shook his head.

'Nowt in t'rules says he can't walk alongside thee lad,' said the umpire.

At the end of his walk back the bowler turned and began his run to the wicket and the old man kept pace with him stride for stride. Halfway to the wicket the bowler stopped.

'Ay up umpire can't tha' see what he's doing,' said the bowler to the umpire at square leg.

'Ay, he's running alongside thee lad but there's nowt to say he can't,' said the umpire.

The bowler shadowed everywhere by my old man completely lost his head and bowled three balls which nearly killed third slip. After the third he turned to my old man and addressed him in what I understood to be called 'pit language'. The old

man listened for a while and then turned to the umpire and said:

'Did tha' hear that Charlie?'

'I did that Sammy,' said Charlie.

'Does tha' reckon it's fit language for a schoolboy to hear?'

'No,' said Charlie firmly.

'Then we're off and claiming maximum points,' said the old man and marched from the field, taking me with him.

As we walked off I pointed out that I had heard that kind of language and worse before so why had he taken umbrage?

'Tactics,' he said.

He proved his case by taking his action to the League Committee and being awarded maximum points for a game we hadn't a hope of winning.

Soon after I left his team to play for Barnsley in the Yorkshire League. But he followed, giving up playing to watch me. When I batted he would stand by the sight screen semaphoring his displeasure onto the field by a series of anguished body contortions. His most spectacular demonstrations always occurred whenever I tried a late cut and missed. He believed firmly with Maurice Leyland that you never late cut before June and even then only if the moon had turned to green cheese. I once played this shot in a game at Barnsley and missed and looked toward the sightscreen where the old man was going through his paroxysm of displeasure. As I watched the stumper approached me.

'Are tha' watching what I'm watching?' he said.

I nodded.

'I reckon he's having a bloody fit,' said the stumper.

Whenever I got near a fifty he couldn't bear to watch and always spent ten minutes in the gents toilet until the crowd noise informed him that I was either on 50 or out. I went to one fifty by hitting the ball into that very same toilet where it was fielded by my old man who came out holding the ball gingerly but looking like a man who has found a gold nugget.

I never told him I didn't want to play cricket for a living. I didn't dare. The truth dawned when I realised a life's ambition and joined 'The Guardian' (Manchester Guardian as it then was). Delightedly I crossed the Pennines to tell my parents. Mother was delighted. Father said:

'It's not like playing cricket for Yorkshire.'

He's not given up. He's now centred all his ambitions on my eldest son. When he was about to be born I was living in Manchester but working in London.

I had reached a perfectly normal and satisfactory arrangement with the Welfare State whereby my firstborn would be delivered into the world in a Lancashire hospital. Sometime near the date of the birth I received a phone call from my father.

'Well it's done then,' he said.

'What is?' I asked.

'I've moved t'wife to a nursing home in Yorkshire,' he said.

'But why, she was perfectly happy in Manchester,' I said.

'Maybe, but we've not only her to think about. What about t'baby?' he said.

'What difference does that make?' I asked.

There was a long pause. He was obviously trying hard to control himself. 'Supposin' it's a boy,' he said.

'I very much hope it is,' I said.

'And if it's born in Lancashire what happens then?' he said.
'Tell me,' I said.

'It can't play for Yorkshire at cricket, that's what,' he yelled,
his temper getting the better of him. 'Anyway like I've told you
I've had them shifted. It's proper thing to do lad.'

A month later there was born in a Wakefield nursing home
my first child, a boy. His name is Andrew and his grandfather
is already convinced that one day he will play for Yorkshire.

All that has gone before is only to explain what it means to
be cricket mad. My old man believes that cricket is the greatest
game in the world. I agree with him. No doubt my sons will
feel the same way. This book is for all those who feel like we
do. In particular it is an offering of love and gratitude to
my old man.

2 A kind of beauty

It always amuses me when people start waxing lyrical about
cricket, reviving all that stuff about blossom-scented air,
dreaming spires, the sound of leather on willow, clergy asleep
in deckchairs. This kind of talk used to worry me when I was
a kid because I knew that cricket wasn't like that, at least not
where I lived.

I remember someone once sent us a calendar which showed
a village cricket field with a thatched boozer at deep fine leg
and a group of men with straw boaters sitting under an ancient
oak sipping tea. For a long time I was sure that the picture was
a fake, a papier maché model erected to the myth of cricket.
It was a long time before I found a ground like it and discovered
the other side of cricket.

Until I did cricket was something which blended into the
landscape of industrial South Yorkshire. Wickets carved out
of spoil heaps, pithead gear poking over the top of the sight
screen, spectators on their haunches around the boundary
chewing grass, spitting advice.

When we travelled away we used old Beckett's taxi, an
ancient and vast Packard which he had found in a lay-by near
Wakefield. The car was Beckett's great love but he couldn't
afford it really. Rather than get rid of it altogether he sold
odd parts of it whenever he needed a few bob. In the last
season he transported us to our away fixtures, the car was

minus headlamps, horn, front and rear bumper bars, rear seat and spare tyre. Once making laborious progress up a gentle slope in Barnsley we were overtaken by a rather elderly lady pushing a pram. This was more than our skipper could take. 'What's up Beckett? There's people walking faster than this car' and Beckett said sadly: 'I know, I know. But tha' sees I've started selling t'engine.'

We finally stopped using him because he became so slow that games fifteen miles away required a dawn start. He finally sold the engine and all the wheels but kept the body propped up on bricks and polished like a guardsman's boots in his allotment.

Our replacement for Beckett's car was a coal lorry which was never cleaned for its human cargo and frequently we would arrive at a ground looking like the black and white minstrels. It was always a relief when we had a home fixture although there was little pleasure in playing on our wicket, unless you happened to be a fast bowler with homicidal tendencies.

There was nothing we could do to improve it. The soil rejected the turf which withered and died and resembled a seedy strip of rush matting, the subsidence caused by the local

mine gave it the even quality of corrugated sheeting. It broke
the heart of every groundsman we ever had except the re-
doubtable Cheyney.   He was a retired miner who kept pigs
and grew roses in his spare time, and had an unswerving faith
in what he called 'nature's cure'.   When he first came to the
club he was shown the wicket by the captain who said: 'What's
tha' reckon Cheyney?' 'Nothing wrong with it that a drop of
nature can't cure,' said Cheyney. 'Nature?' said the captain.
'Ay nature,' said Cheyney, ''oss muck, pig muck. You know,
manure.'

For the next few days Cheyney was observed carting vast
quantities of 'nature' to the ground and smearing it across the
wicket. On match day it had set like concrete and looked true
enough.

'Told you,' said Cheyney. 'Now't like a bit of 'oss muck.'

His triumph was short-lived because it rained and the pitch
turned to an evil smelling glue. The captain shouted at Cheyney
about the smell, Cheyney answered back to the effect that
farmyard smells were healthy and that if the captain doubted
it he should inspect his roses. Before we knew it we were
advertising for another groundsman.

In the end we decided to have the whole square relaid, a
singularly expensive business which took three years of beetle
drives, dances and collections to achieve. On the great day the
ground looked a picture. The new turf was a springy green
carpet, the crowd large and noisy in its honour. The first ball
of the new square was received by our captain in recognition
of his sterling work. It was a delivery of no great pace which
pitched just short of a length and hit our captain straight
between the eyes. The firm who made the pitch had created a
monster. It was worse than the one it replaced. There was
nothing we could do about it but adapt our styles to our
predicament. The trouble was that although there are many
books on cricket which explain to the last detail how to play
every known shot, there's none which advises the young
cricketer how to avoid decapitation.

We went about solving our problems in our own peculiar ways. I favoured a shimmy to square leg as the bowler delivered and was able to defend this graceless and cowardly manoeuvre by stating that Bradman had used it against Larwood. My old man favoured more subtle means. Being ambidextrous he would take one delivery as a right-handed batsman and then change over for the next one. He explained that this ploy prevented the bowler getting him in his sights. Moreover, he relied heavily on his reputation as a fast bowler who believed in meeting fire with fire.

I well remember batting with him on one occasion when he was given a going over by a youth who had more energy than sense. Having hit the old man for the umpteenth time he thought it time to apologise. 'Sorry,' he grunted. 'Don't apologise lad,' said the old man with a disarming smile. 'It's my turn next and I won't apologise when I hit thee.' And he was as good as his word.

All this was a long time ago and a long way removed from the popular notion of cricket in England. Slag heaps instead of cathedrals, cloth caps instead of straw hats, bared teeth instead of polite smiles. Not idyllic I must admit, but it had its own kind of beauty.

3 Let battle commence

My cricket seasons always began at Bramall Lane, Sheffield, in
Stygian gloom, with the clouds so low they sat on the football
stands and we seemed to be playing in a darkened corridor.
Those dreamers who see cricket as a sunlit game with creamy
figures flitting hither and thither throwing graceful shadows
should try Bramall Lane in April.

Those who are prepared to face the truth could not wish a
better introduction. First there was the wicket itself. The
rumour is that they don't cut the grass in Sheffield, just roll it
flat. And certainly one could bring forward as evidence many
cricketers, all sober men with 20/20 vision, who would swear
to having seen the grass rising in front of them in the opening
overs of a game. Ordinarily it wouldn't matter too much,
but it made a deal of difference when we played at Bramall
Lane because it meant we had to face George Pope.

Given a combination of the new ball, a succulent wicket and
the clouds low and heavy George Pope, on an April afternoon
in Sheffield, was capable of bowling out any side in the world.
He was, of course, one of the most devastating seam bowlers
ever reared in Derbyshire, which is another way of saying he
was one of the best in the world. To face him in the first few
minutes of a brand new season was an experience comparable
to being beaten with a soft cosh on the day you were born. It
left you with no illusions about the future.

I played against him for four seasons in these circumstances, which explains why I love cricket as a cynical bitch of a mistress instead of the crinolined lady most people take her for.

It wasn't just George Pope's absolute mastery of the art of bowling that taught you the whole lesson, it was also his complete understanding of cricket psychology. Once, after being clobbered for a magnificent six by a brave and unrazored youth Pope remarked with a benign smile 'They go a lot further when you middle them sonny.' He then brought up an extra short leg and bowled him next ball. His manipulation of umpires is worth a chapter in any book on psychology.

It would start as soon as they met in the middle.

'Good day, Mr. Umpire,' said George.

'Good day, George,' said the umpire, slightly flattered at being singled out by the great man.

'Not very pleasant for the time of year,' said George.

'Terrible.'

'I always say that you chaps earn your money turning out in stuff like this. And how's the lumbago?' asked George.

'Playing up a bit thank you,' said the umpire, surprised he should know about it.

'And how are your roses this year?' George asked.

'Look very promising,' said the umpire, by now beside himself with joy that this man should be so concerned with both his passions and his problems.

From then on the batsman was doomed.

The first time Pope hit the pads, usually with a massive in-swinger that would have finished life at square leg, he would turn to the umpire, smile and say:

'Not quite, I think, not quite.'

The next time there would be a strangled appeal from George and an immediate apology. 'Sorry Mr. Umpire, again not quite. You were quite right to ignore me.'

The umpire was still congratulating himself on his exquisite judgment when George would strike again, but this time with an appeal you could hear in Manchester.

And this time the umpire, who by now was so fond of George he was entertaining thoughts of adopting him, would put his finger up. It never failed. The only consolation to the batsman was that it really didn't make much different because had Pope not chosen to get you LBW in that particular way, he could have bowled you any time he wanted to.

The fact that George Pope is now a county umpire is the classic instance of a poacher turning gamekeeper.

Our encounter with Pope at Bramall Lane always developed into verbal battles of rare quality between him and Ellis Robinson. Robinson was our professional. He had played cricket for Yorkshire and Somerset and was an off-spinner of imagination and real skill.

The classic Robinson-Pope meeting came the Saturday after Blackpool had beaten Bolton in the cup final. Bramall Lane that day was a seductive, lush strip of turf made to measure for George Pope and his art and he didn't conceal his delight when Sheffield won the toss and sent us in.

'Fancy thi' chances then Ellis,' he yelled through our dressing room door.

'I'll gi' thee some stick this afternoon Popey. Ah can bat thee wi' mi' cap neb,' replied Ellis.

But it was Popey's day and not all of Robinson's optimism or skill could prevent it.

Ellis came in about fourth wicket down with few runs on the board and Popey swinging them like boomerangs.

He walked slowly to the crease, taking his time, adjusting his eyes to the light, sizing things up. He took guard, touched his Yorkshire cap and looked hard at Popey standing in the slips. 'Na' then Ellis, are tha' going to get any chalks?'

'Reckon on 50 George.'

'I'm doing a bit today tha' knows Ellis.'

'Tha' nivver could bowl.'

Robinson settles into his stance. The bowler begins his run. Tap-tap, bat on crease. An outswinger, Robinson forward. Misses. Stumper takes it.

Pope (looking up at heaven): 'Jesus Christ Ellis. Tha' allus wor lucky.'

'Lucky be buggered. I let the bloody thing past.'

'Nivver. Nivver. Tha' nivver saw it.'

And so on, until Pope was bowling which prevented him from talking, but not Robinson who now conversed with which ever fielder happened to be the nearest.

'Fancy thi' chances does tha' lad? Be careful. I wouldn't like to face meself on this track today. Not today I wouldn't. Oh no.'

Pope approaching the crease. Loose, almost affable action. Not so quick as he used to be but twice as crafty. Right to the far edge of the bowling crease. Immaculate length. Ball pushed diagonally at the leg stump. A lot of cut on it. Hits pitch and snaps back, beats the bat and catches Robinson high on the front pad as he pushes forward Pope whips around, glowers at the umpire for a second and then lets one go which rattles the pavilion windows.

'Owzat?'

'Not out,' says the umpire.

'And I should bloody well think not,' shouts Robinson from the other end of the pitch, 'it wouldn't have hit a set of stumps six feet high.'

Pope glares at him down the track. Robinson glares back. There seems to be no one else in the whole of Bramall Lane except these two glaring and snarling at one another.

Pope turns on his heel and walks back to his mark. As he passes the umpire who is still trembling from the blast of the appeal, he says, in a soft, polite voice, 'A little high perhaps Mr. Umpire?'

The umpire nods.

'Perhaps so,' says George, all smooth and buttery, 'but I thought I would enquire, you know.'

And so it went on. There was no holding Pope that day. Everything was right for him: the grass, green and damp and gripping the seam like a lover, making the ball change direction as if it had a mind of its own.

We were bowled out for under 50 and Pope took eight wickets for less than 20 runs. Our only reassurance was that he would have taken wickets against any team in the world on that track and in those conditions.

We were in with a chance with Robinson angry and a couple of useful seamers. But it rained during the tea interval and when play recommenced the wicket was wet and useless and Sheffield easily knocked off the runs. It was no good talking to Robinson as we changed for home. He kept muttering to himself, 'Bloody weather. I'd have shown Popey. Nivver could bowl. I'd have caused some panic.'

So we went into the bar to drown our sorrows and went home silently, in our special bus through the rain-misty, slimy streets of Sheffield with only a stop for a fish and six and a bag of scraps before we reached Barnsley.

We went to our own club bar where we told the second team just how much Popey had been bending them—exaggerating like anglers—until Saturday night slid away into Sunday morning when we woke up stiff as sergeant majors, certain now that the season had started. And glad.

4 Doing it for money

The basic difference between the Southern and Northern cricketer is that one does it for money and the other for free. The fact that the Northern club cricketer is more serious about his game is partly due to breeding but more to do with the fact that a good performance with bat or ball will gain him a collection. This sytem of passing the hat round for someone who had made fifty or taken five wickets is in many ways the cornerstone of North Country cricket. It gives it a unique flavour, it turns Saturday afternoon sportsmen into hard-eyed professionals. There are Northern cricketers renowned as 'collection players'. These are the men who can guarantee that their Saturday evening booze-up will be paid for by the spectators. The best one I ever played with devoted his entire life to a study of the science of collection cricket. His comments about the weather were all to do with money.

'Good collection weather' he would say as the sun blazed down on the cricket field. After changing into his whites he would often go down to the turnstile to welcome the paying customers, rubbing his hands in the most obsequious manner, behaving like a head waiter. The simile is accurate because like a head waiter he was touting for tips. When he came back to the pavilions we'd ask: 'What's the crowd like Charlie?' 'Ten pounds twelve and six worth,' he'd say. This was Charlie's estimate of what the first collection would yield. He was never more than sixpence wrong. The collection was the best barometer of public opinion ever invented. It told the player precisely how much or how little he had entertained the spectators. My maiden fifty in club cricket left me elated. I returned to the pavilion like a champion, drunk with my talents, eager to gain my reward. 'How much?' I asked the skipper who was always entrusted with the collection. He pointed to the table where lay the contents of the collection boxes. The crowd had assessed my innings as being worth fourteen and sevenpence halfpenny made up entirely in halfpennies, two brass buttons, one blue tiddlywink and a badge which said I was now a member of the Flash Gordon Fan Club.

It was my introduction to the most honest criticism a player can ever have. People could flatter you with false words but when they were asked to put their money where their mouth was they spoke the truth. The criticism of the collection system is that it rewards individuals in what is essentially a team game. That is what the purists say, but I've always thought that cricket is the most selfish of games and that the collection system doesn't corrupt anyone; it is simply an honest antidote to all that bilge about playing for the sake of the club, country and general well-being of the soul. Once you've won a collection the money is yours to do with as you like; the only time you are expected to relinquish your loot is during a benefit game. Then the rule is that all collections are donated to the beneficiary who will then leave ten quid or so behind the bar for the team to get drunk on.

Benefit games are the cricketer's gold watch, an expression of gratitude by club and spectators to a player who has sacrificed most important things, including his wife and his liver, for their enjoyment.

Sometimes, though, they can go very wrong indeed. And when a benefit game turns nasty the difference between that and a normally keen cricket match is the difference between a tap-room brawl with broken bottles and a pillow fight in the dormitory.

I still carry the scars from one of these games. It occurred
in those dear tender days when my only problem was deciding
whether I'd like to be Keith Miller or Neville Cardus. I was
playing for a team in the North and we agreed to stage a
benefit game for a batsman who was the idol of the county.
We had in the team at the time a gnarled old professional who
had once played for the county and was now forced to earn
his pennies in the leagues. He was a talented cricketer, a good
enough spin bowler to have gone through the Australians on
one occasion. But he never quite made the top.

His benefit year with the county had coincided with the
monsoon season and he'd been kicked out of the game shortly
after with a lot of memories and no money. He nursed his
disenchantment savagely but quietly, until he got drunk, which
was often, or until he had an off day and bowled badly, and
then his fielders were showered with a rich and most original
flow of abuse.

In one game he was pummelled by a large and unorthodox
batsman who reckoned nothing to our professional's reputation nor his subtle snares of flight and spin. He simply put his
front foot forward and thumped the ball with a frightening
noise to all parts of the ground. Not to be bested our pro
simply moved the leg trap closer. 'Gerrin closer. He can't
ruddy well bat,' he would say as they retrieved the ball from
the tennis courts.

I was the centre of the leg trap and frighteningly close. The
batsman eyed me and grinned, 'Tha' for t'morgue standing
theer,' he said pleasantly. And he was nearly right. He swung
at the next ball, I ducked covering all my important parts and
was struck a horrifying crack on the knee cap. The ball shot
off my knee (I thought it had gone clean through it) to the
boundary.

I lay there crippled wondering if I were alive or not when I
saw our pro glowering down at me. 'What's matter, lightning?'
he said. I muttered something about my knee and a doctor
whereupon he said, bitterly, 'Tha' doesn't want medical
treatment, tha' wants stuffin'.' It wasn't that he particularly

disliked me. He treated everyone he played with or against with the same detached hostility.

Anyway he didn't want to play in this benefit game because he said he did not like the beneficiary. He was probably jealous because his benefit was a disaster and the man whose game he was asked to play in had already made a fortune out of cricket. But he was made to play. The captain and the committee insisted, which, as it turned out, was the worst decision they ever made.

The day of the game was perfect, the crowd large and ready to spend and the beneficiary arrived looking prosperous and happy. This joyful combination simply made our pro spend longer than usual in the bar before the game 'lubricating the arm', as he put it. By the time we took the field he was muttering gently to himself. Later someone said he was saying 'I'll fix 'im' over and over to himself, but that might be a case of inventing the quote after the event.

All went well for a while. The runs came briskly, our pro allowed himself to be thumped without recourse to violence on his colleagues and everyone was thinking what a pleasant occasion it was. Then came the moment the crowd had waited for. One of the openers was bowled by our pro and out came the beneficiary.

The crowd rose to him and cheered as he walked to the wicket. He looked around at them smiling and no doubt adding up how much a fifty would be worth. He arrived at the wicket and settled in to take first ball. Now the golden rule of benefit games is that the beneficiary is given an easy first ball to get him off the mark and feeling happy. The great batsman waited for the gift to be granted. But our pro ran up and bowled him the best off-break it has ever been anyone's misfortune to face. It pitched off stump to a good length, bit, spun sharply, turned inside the bat and flattened the leg stump. It would have bowled anyone in the world.

For a moment there was absolute, unbelieving silence on the ground. The batsmen looked poleaxed, our captain starting going purple, the fielders hung their heads in embarrassment.

The only person on the ground who looked pleased was our pro. He was standing by the umpire giggling gently to himself. There looked to be no solution. The great man had to go, bowled first ball in his benefit game. Fully 30 seconds had elapsed before the umpire at square leg came up with the answer. As the great batsman turned to walk away he shouted: 'No ball.'

Our pro stopped giggling and gaped in disbelief. Our captain knocked the leg stump back in, patted the great batsman on the back, and relegated our pro to the outfield where he spent the rest of the afternoon sulking. The great batsman, recovered now from the shock, went on to make fifty and the incident was forgotten until the tea interval when our skipper bawled out the pro for his misbehaviour.

But the pro's great moment was yet to come. After the game we gathered in the bar for the ritual of counting the money. There it was on the table, mountains of silver and copper. The Chairman announced that about £300 had been collected.

This pleased us because form demanded that he leave at least £20 behind the bar so that the rest of us could get drunk at his expense. We had all worked up a splendid thirst when the great batsman arrived to collect his loot. He walked into the bar, scooped all the money into a small potato sack, shook hands with the chairman of the committee and walked out. No beer money, not even a thank you. We sat there hurt and angry by his ingratitude. For a long time nobody said a word and then the skipper turned to our pro and said 'Did tha' mean to bowl him first ball?'

'I did that,' said the pro.

'It wor a good un,' said our skipper nodding his head.

'Good enough,' said our pro.

'Come to think of it, it were just about the best ball I've ever seen,' said the skipper. And we all nodded wisely and settled into an evening of yarning and drinking, at our own expense. Later, after playing club cricket in the South I returned North and saw our professional. He asked me what kind of season I'd had and I told him I'd done quite well and made a few fifties. 'You'll be in the money then lad,' he said. I told him that they didn't have collections in the South. He stared at me in disbelief. 'No collections?' he said. I shook my head. 'Then the game's not worth playing is it?' he said. I agreed and I think I still do. I know that the pleasure of cricket is supposedly stored in the soul, but how much more pleasant if a little bit is also stashed in the bank.

5 The next man in is Walter Mitty

The nice thing about sport is that it brings out the Walter Mitty in all of us. From time to time I have opened for England with Boycott and rattled up a double century before lunch, beaten Jean Claude Killy with ridiculous ease in the Winter Olympics and regularly ridden a 100 to 1 outsider to spectacular victory in the Derby. This last one is my favourite fantasy because according to my dreams both the horse and the key to my heart are owned by a titled lady of great beauty and after my win we drink champagne and nibble goodies in her penthouse suite and she whispers softly to me: 'How do you do it Parky?' And I with becoming nonchalance reply: 'Really my lady it was nothing.'

Such dreams are beautiful and harmless. They only turn nasty when you try and make them come true. For instance even though I am confident that I could win Wimbledon any time I want I would never actually join the competition and take my chance against Laver and the like. I would rather sit at home in front of my television set nursing my superiority. Not all sports fantasists are as sensible. For instance a 55 year old American, Mr. Homer Shoop, carried all his fantasies into real life when he partnered Gardner Mulloy in the veteran men's doubles at Wimbledon. There he stood on the number five court, partnered by a man who had once been tennis champion of America, ready to prove to all the world that Homer Shoop was a name to rank with the immortals of tennis.

Sadly and predictably, Mr. Shoop had his dream shattered. The game, by his own admission, was 'ridiculous'. He and his partner lost 6-1, 6-4, the crowd laughed at them and Gardner Mulloy described what happened as a 'real pantomime' and a 'humiliation'. The unfortunate Homer Shoop did his best to restore his tattered dignity, by explaining, 'I had bad 'flu, a very bad left knee and a weak right wrist.'

Homer Shoop was not the first sportsman to fall foul of his dreams. I once played cricket with a young man who dreamed of being the Reverend David Sheppard. The fact that his real name was Horace, that he lived in the South Yorkshire coal-field, and that his Dad was regularly in the pawnshop with the old woman's wedding ring only increased his desire to become a gentleman cricketer of impeccable breeding. Nor was he deterred by the fact that he was a very ordinary cricketer trying to emulate one of the best batsmen in the world. He studied Sheppard in action for hours and practised in front of a mirror until he had managed an exact copy of that great batsman's stance at the wicket. He even copied Sheppard's hairstyle and mode of dress but failed at that too. When the rest of us were resplendent in slim jims, winklepickers, tight pants and crew cuts he would turn up looking like a grotesque parody of Bertie Wooster.

Nothing could dissuade Horace from his dream. One day, after he had ordered a dry Martini in the spitting ring of a boozer in Barnsley and received a derisive sneer from the bar-man, I said to him: 'Look, wouldn't it be easier if you became Freddie Trueman or Len Hutton or someone like that. Some-one a bit nearer your own background?' He gave me a sad smile and sipped what in Barnsley passes for a dry Martini. 'My dear Michael, you simply don't understand. This Sheppard chappie stands for everything I envy. Poise, breeding, talent. It's all there, old chap. You can't do better than copy a master, after all,' he said. I knew then it was hopeless, that nothing short of brain surgery would change his fantasy.

On the whole his friends and team mates came to learn how to live with him. The important exception was our captain who had an immense contempt for anyone who couldn't drink fifteen pints without falling down and a firm belief that God had a Yorkshire accent. He treated Horace with an undisguised hostility. The flashpoint in their relationship occurred during a game when they were batting together. We were in need of quick runs, a tactical consideration which Horace placed second to his impersonation of David Sheppard. After playing an elegant on-drive through mid-wicket he maintained the final position, carefully checking that the shot was a perfect replica of Sheppard's and oblivious to the fact that the captain was galloping up and down the wicket like a runaway tram. The captain had completed two runs and was about to set off on a risky third when he suddenly realised that Horace had not moved and was still engrossed in a painstaking survey of his shot.

Our captain inspected the immaculate statue at the other end of the wicket and, after a moment's hesitation, set off towards him. It looked as if he decided there was a run to be had, but I believe he had murder in his mind, that his target was not the opposite crease but a point somewhere between Horace's eyes. At this moment Horace awoke from his reverie, saw the skipper charging down the wicket, saw the ball winging in from the outfield and with an imperious gesture held up his hand and shouted, in what he took to be an upper class drawl, 'No. Get back, skipper.'

'I'll gi' thi' get back yer great Nancy,' yelled the skipper charging towards him. At which point Horace took the decision which undeniably saved his life. As the skipper closed on him, bat raised, he set off in vain pursuit of the other crease. He was run out by several yards and retired to the pavilion trying to be very public school about it. Our captain went on to make fifty and get a collection, which probably accounted for the fact that he didn't strangle Horace on his return to the pavilion. It was shortly after this incident that Horace had his dreams cruelly and finally shattered. He was by this time so well known in the league that he was a natural target for those fast bowlers

whose one reaction to eccentricity of any kind was a well-directed bumper. Horace's ambition to be a gentleman and play at Lord's with his hero was taken from him by a swarthy paceman from Rotherham who distinctly heard Horace say, 'Spiffing shot,' after he had square-cut him to the boundary. The next ball was short of a length and of immense pace. It lifted from the wicket like a missile and struck Horace full in the groin.

As he lay there all pretence left him. He was no longer David Sheppard but Horace from the backs who had been painfully felled. He relieved his agony with a colourful description of the bowler and his family. The language was not the kind you would expect from someone who had read a book on etiquette, nor did the accent signify expensive elocution lessons in Wakefield. At the end of the tirade, our opening bat said to him jokingly, 'The Reverend David Sheppard wouldn't have said that Horace.' Horace looked at him balefully. '. . . David Sheppard,' he said, simply.

It was the end of his dream and we did our best to console him. He gave up cricket at the end of that season and after a

brief period, where he flirted with the idea of being Luis
Miguel Dominguin, dropped out of the fantasy business altogether. He had learned the lesson that it is safer to keep your
sporting fantasies locked in the mind.

I have in my time been Lew Hoad, Freddie Trueman,
Stirling Moss, Bobby Charlton, Lester Piggott, Roger Ban-
nister, and Rockfist Rogan, the two-fisted wonder. I have won
Test matches single-handed, ridden Derby winners, broken
several world records on the running track and won the men's
singles at Wimbledon more times than any other person.
Once I even managed to become Mary Rand without being
arrested. The trick is to keep it in your mind. It's my secret that
beneath this unremarkable exterior there lurks a world-beater.

6 Hero in a jock strap

I know a man who's never got over the fact that he once sat
next to someone in a train who, the night before, had been in
a boozer with a bloke who said he knew Len Hutton. The
man who told me this story told it not once but many times,
and on each occasion his eyes popped like chapel hat pegs at
the glory of the moment.

This of course is a common symptom among those who
follow any sport. To love a game is to exaggerate its players to
jumbo size. It means you make heroes of them and see them
through magic eyeballs. The dearest wish of any sports lover,
no matter what his age, is to meet his heroes and thereby get
one toe inside the Pantheon.

When I was a kid I saw Wilfred Rhodes, in his seventies,
totally blind but with a back as straight as a young tree, being
led gently to his place at the Scarborough cricket festival. He
had come to hear the cricket and as he passed people stood up
and smiled, and doffed their hats and said, 'Ayup Wilfred,
lad.' He nodded all the time, hearing them but not seeing them.

Stuffed as I was with his legends I had no eyes for the
match. I simply sat as near to him as I could and watched
him. An old man in knobbly tweeds and blind but still a God.
I heard him speak. He said something about the weather.
Back at the boarding house where we were staying I told the
owner's son that I had that day seen Wilfred Rhodes and
heard him speak.

'Who's Wilfred Rhodes?' he said. So next year we changed boarding houses.

But on the whole the fortunate hero worshippers are those who never get near enough to their heroes to have their dreams defiled by disenchantment. When I was a reporter on a local paper I persuaded the editor to let me write a profile for our junior page on a cricketer who, at the time, was the darling of the county and the world. The editor thought it was a good idea, provided I did it in my spare time, paid my own bus fare to and from the ground and didn't forget to collect the whist drive winners on the way back.

So it was I found myself in the dressing-room thirty minutes before the day's play started, surrounded with the men I had worshipped all my life.

My great hero and the subject of the profile was standing on a chair looking out from the dressing-room window. He was wearing nothing but boots and a very short vest and I noticed, as you do, that he had a large spot at the back of his left knee which he kept scratching with the toe of his right boot. He was looking through binoculars. I remained in awed silence. The Great Cricketer was obviously searching the wicket for signs of imperfection or scanning the horizon for weather clues. He spoke:

'That red-head's back again,' he said to a player standing next to him. This player was wearing his cap and a jock strap.

'She'd tek on a platoon of guardsmen that one,' said jock strap.

A pause while the Great Cricketer scratched his spot and adjusted his focus.

'Bloody hell. Tek a look at that one.'

'One in blue?'

'Ay.'

'Not seen her before.'

'No.'

'What's tha' reckon?' asked the Great Cricketer.

'Bet she's a reight goer,' said jock strap.

The Great Cricketer paused, scratched his backside and said 'That's it then. Bat first, quick fifty, shower, fast rub down wi't 'Sporting Life' and she's mine.'

Having thus planned his innings he turned and saw me for the first time. 'And what's tha' want kid?' he asked.

I told him what the idea was. I said we wanted a story to give inspiration to our young readers.

'How much?' he asked.

I said, tremblingly, that I didn't quite understand.

'How much bloody money for t'piece?' he demanded.

I pointed out feebly that our paper was not in the habit of paying interviewees. He started scowling. Perhaps, I added quickly, I could make do with a single quote (for free, of course), a short piece of advice on how young cricketers might achieve his kind of greatness.

He thought a bit, then said: 'Ay, I'll gi' thee a piece of good advice. Always be polite to women and don't go sleeping in wet grass. Now shove off.'

So I went. I was so shattered I forgot to collect the whist drive winners and got bawled out by the editor. But I got my revenge that same night by taking the Great Cricketer's name out of my World Eleven to play Mars.

Now the point is that to anyone less resilient than myself that sort of incident could cause irreparable harm. All it did to me, however, was broaden my mean streak.

There are some people however who would hear no evil of their heroes, not even if they found them beating up old people and pinching their pensions. I have a friend like this. One day, a few seasons ago, he brought his ten-year-old son along to a charity cricket match I was playing in. The star attraction was a Great Bowler who was very tight-lipped on this occasion because there wasn't any free booze and, as he pointed out, he only got ten quid for playing in charity games.

Anyway I was sitting next to him on the pavilion balcony when the ten-year-old son of this friend of mine approached the Great Bowler.

'Could I have your autograph please, Sir?' he asked.

The Great Bowler was looking hard at the birds in their summer dresses.

'Get stuffed,' he said.

Ever eager to start a fight between other people, I recounted this story straightaway to the boy's father. He listened intently.

'Is that really what he said?' he asked. I avowed it was an accurate report of the affair as I had witnessed it.

'What a character!' he said with a huge smile.

He now tells that story to his friends as proof of just what a card the Great Bowler is. Funny people, sports lovers. But not half so funny as their heroes.

7 The rain was terrestial

The most fascinating study in snob-sport is cricket. Whether or not you are a snob about the game is largely a matter of geography. If you were born within spitting distance of Lords the odds are strongly in favour of your growing up to be a snob about the game, whereas anyone reared north of the nineteenth hole at Potters Bar Golf Course is likely to have a much broader philosophy. This conflict between north and south, which has provided cricket with some of its more memorable moments, is all about snobbery. The north-country player reared on rough cricket regards his southern counterpart as a toffee-nosed twit. Similarly the southern cricketer, brought up to believe that the game is simply a good way of working up a thirst, looks north with horror at the flannelled barbarians.

All the best cricket stories are about the northern lad doing down the southern snob. I could only have been a dozen years old when I received my first instruction in how to deal with the enemy. I was being coached by an old Yorkshire cricketer who was explaining the art of bowling. 'Bowling's about length and direction. None of this fancy stuff. Bowl straight and pitch a length. T'only time tha' forgets this golden rule is when tha'rt faced by one of them fancy buggers wi' a striped cap. Then tha' forgets what I've just telled thi' and aims straight for his head,' he said.

The north country archetype in these stories about snob conflict in cricket is F. S. Trueman. Throughout his career he

BEFORE AFTER

has waged constant war against the airs and graces of the snob cricketer. His task has been made easy in that next to the zebra the snob cricketer is easily the most identifiable animal in the world. He is likely to wear a multi-coloured striped cap, hold up his trousers with a multi-coloured tie and when thinking about a single often addresses his partner thus:

'Just the jolly one on this occasion Charles, I think.'

There is a famous Trueman story about his encounter with just such a cricketer. It occurred in Trueman's sapling days when the sight of a snob cricketer made him bowl twenty miles an hour faster than normal. This particular young man faced Trueman and was completely beaten by a delivery of such pace and venom that it reduced his stumps to a smouldering ruin. As he passed the scowling Trueman he remembered his manners and said: 'That was a jolly fine delivery, my man.'

Trueman glowered at him and then said: 'Ay it was that. But it was bloody well wasted on thee.'

It is not everyone who remains as dedicated to the battle as Trueman. Some cricketers sell out and attempt to join the snob set. In the main the attempts have been disastrous. The first sign that a cricketer is about to go over to the enemy is when he starts speaking posh. I played for a team in Yorkshire skippered by a man who was never the same after standing in a lift next to E. W. Swanton. From that day on he dedicated his life to becoming a snob cricketer. Unfortunately he couldn't afford elocution lessons and his attempts at self-education were laughable. He simply didn't know what to do with his aitches. He stopped play in one game with an example of his own version of the Oxford accent. The incident was provoked by a slow left-arm bowler called Alf who was notoriously cowardly against attacking batsmen. Even on wickets that suited spin he would revert to medium pace seamers if his opponent seemed likely to chance his arm against the slow stuff. On this particular occasion he was bowling his slow stuff on a wicket taking a lot of spin. In desperation one of the batsmen made a couple of suicidal strokes and scored two desperate boundaries. Immediately Alf started bowling at medium pace. Our captain watched this tactic with growing impatience and finally bellowed:

'H'oh for 'eaven's sake h'Alf give 'em some bloody h'air . . .'

A long pause while captain and Alf glowered at one another and then:

'H'idiot.'

Fred Trueman tells a similar story of a Yorkshire cricketer who began to get ideas above his station after being awarded his England cap. The trip to Lords changed him completely and he returned to play for his county entertaining thoughts of marrying the daughter of the President of MCC. On the morning of his first match with the county after playing for England he looked out of the bedroom window and said:

'The rain is terrestial.'

His team mate looked dumbfounded.

'Surely tha' means torrential,' he said.

The new England player shrugged his shoulders. 'It's all imperial to me,' he said.

The curious thing about snob cricketers is that for all they preach about good manners and sportsmanship they can turn very nasty when aroused. As a very junior national service officer in the Army I once captained a team of Other Ranks against a team of Senior Officers.

The captain of the opposition was the adjutant, a snob cricketer of amazing calibre. I set about devising a plan to disturb his finery, ruffle his feathers. What I came up with was, I admit, fairly nasty. It involved the use of a simple and aggressive soul from Sheffield who was wasting his National Service in the cookhouse. He was quick enough to play good League cricket in Yorkshire and daft enough not to mind whom he hit. I told him that if he pinned the adjutant to the sight screen he was on as much beer as he could drink and no extra duties for two weeks.

Came the day with the tents up and all the camp watching. The adjutant's team won the toss and batted on a wicket officially described as 'sporting' by everyone except those unfortunate enough to bat on it. The adjutant opened and looked rather beautiful. He wore one of those caps with multi-coloured rings, and a silk muffler.

I gave the ball to the lad from Sheffield, reminded him of his duties, and put four men up close on the leg side.

'A touch of the old leg theory?' said the adjutant.

I pretended not to hear.

The first ball pitched just short of a length and flicked the adjutant's muffler as it flashed by. The adjutant gave the bowler the look he reserved for recalcitrant natives. The next three balls had him ducking and weaving like a cornfield in a high wind. The crunch came with the fifth delivery. A pig. It leapt vertically at the adjutant's head. He shoved his bat at it, the ball cracked his fingers and lobbed gently to one of the short legs who caught it.

The adjutant dropped his bat, rubbed his fingers and commenced swearing in the most officerly way.

'Not too painful?' I inquired. He glowered.

The bowler from Sheffield, as all fast bowlers from the area are taught to do, snarled at his victim from the opposite end of the pitch.

Eventually the adjutant recovered, but instead of walking he stood his ground.

I said, 'You're out.'

The bowler said: 'Get back in t'ruddy hutch' (which is simply another way of saying the same thing).

The adjutant said: 'I suggest you consult the umpire.'

So we did.

'Not out,' said the umpire, who had been recruited from a local club side.

'Why?' I asked.

'No ball,' he said.

'But you didn't call it,' I said.

'No. But I have now,' he said, with a sneer.

There could be no further argument. The bowler from Sheffield went berserk, lost his control and was carted all over the field. The adjutant scored 50 and we lost. After the game the bowler called the umpire a dozy devil in front of the adjutant and was shortly after posted in what seemed mysterious circumstances to a remote island in the Indian Ocean. The incident beautifully summarised the conflicts and tensions that make cricket such a special game. The class war may be dying down in various sectors of our society but it is still very much alive on the cricket fields of England.

8 John Willy Jardine

I once played for a team captained by a man who thought he was Douglas Jardine. The fact that his name was John Willy and the team he captained swam in the lower reaches of Yorkshire league cricket did nothing to dissuade the impersonation. He even went to the lengths of buying himself a multi-coloured cricket cap of the sort that Jardine favoured, which in the area where we played, constituted an act of unsurpassed bravery. The cap was finally taken from him in the most innocent circumstances, when one Christmas John Willy arrived hom from the pit to find it sodden and dejected, sitting atop the snowman erected by his children in their back yard. He was never the same without it.

Of all the captains I have played with he was the most impressive, the hardest, the most imaginative, and I first came across him shortly after leaving school and joining my first league side. In the coal lorry going to the match he explained the subtleties of playing in this particular class of cricket.

'Now tha' sees first thing is t'new ball. There's nowt fancy in this league, we get a new ball every Barnsley Feast so tha' has to be thinking all t'time abart when it might come and how tha' gets thi' hands on it first,' he said. He explained that he was only telling us this because he had heard that the team we were to play that afternoon had bought a new ball recently and he reckoned they were saving it for us. That being the

case it was important to the outcome of the game that we get
our hands on it first.

We arrived at the ground and were changing when the
opposing captain came into our dressing room. He was the
local headmaster and therefore not very popular with John
Willy who thought teachers were layabouts.

'Good afternoon John Willy, lovely day,' said the headmaster.

John Willy was never a man for pleasantries. 'I hear tha'
bought a new ball,' he said. The headmaster smiled blandly.
'You have been misinformed John Willy. This is the match
ball.' He produced a battered piece of leather which looked as
if it had suffered a lifetime being bounced on concrete wickets.
John Willy nodded and said nothing. He went out with the
headmaster, won the toss and elected to bat. As he strapped
his pads on and prepared to open the innings he said to us:

'Yon teacher's trying summat on. Ah reckon he's got t'new
ball in his pocket. If it happens that he brings it out when
play starts, then I want you all to stand down by yon hedge
at square leg. First chance I get I'll thump t'ball down theer
and I don't want it to come back. Understand?' We nodded.

Sure enough, as the opening bowler measured out his run
the headmaster, with a superior smirk handed him a shiny,
red new ball. Halfway through the first over John Willy lay
back and pulled the ball hard towards the square leg boundary
where it crashed into the hedge. After ten minutes of fruitless
searching the umpires, who were worried about the game
running into licensing hours, ordered the headmaster to re-
start the game using the battered old ball we had seen in the
pavilion.

Back in the dressing room someone said, 'Who found it?'
Our slow bowler put his hand up. 'Wheer is it then?' someone
asked. 'Down a bloody rabbit hole' said the slow bowler.
Overjoyed by his tactical triumph, John Willy played an
inspired innings, and when we declared with about 160 on the
board he had scored an unbeaten ninety-odd. He came in the
dressing room pink with self-satisfaction. 'That's what tha'

calls strategy,' he said to the room. 'Now then, wheer's t'new ball.' 'Down a rabbit hole,' said the slow bowler. 'Wheer?' asked John Willy, his face clouding. The slow bowler repeated what he had said. John Willy by this time was trying hard to control himself. Finally he addressed the slow bowler: 'Then go and get t'bloody thing from t'bloody rabbit hole and polish it up nice and shiny.'

Mercifully the slow bowler located the rabbit hole and found the new ball. Polishing it on his backside John Willy went round to the opposition's dressing room and said to the captain, 'By a stroke of good luck we've managed to find t'proper match ball. I tek it tha's no objection to us using it.' The headmaster, aware he had come up against a superior tactician, shook his head sullenly. Armed with the new ball we got them all out for less than fifty. 'Strategy, that's what tha' needs in this game,' John Willy kept saying, and I came to regard him with the kind of hero worship I had reserved up until that time for The Wolf of Kabbul and Baldy Hogan.

I was with him the day he perished and it was a fitting end to such an unorthodox career. John Willy was batting in a local derby game which contained more than the usual amount of needle when he fell victim to one of cricket's more out-rageous whims. He snicked a ball very hard on to his body whereupon it somehow burst through the flies of his trousers and settled inside his pants just above his knee. The wicket keeper and the bowler, sensing an easy wicket and undue humiliation for John Willy, set off toward him with the intention of rescuing the ball while John Willy went through an incredible pantomime trying to extract it and throw it on the ground.

Undeterred by John Willy's dire warnings about what might happen to them if they laid a finger on him, the wicket keeper and the fast bowler both made a purposeful approach toward their victim. What happened next is a matter for dispute. Some say John Willy chinned the fast bowler with a left hook, some say the fast bowler knocked himself out by running on to John Willy's elbow just as the batsman was extracting the

ball. Whatever the circumstances, the fast bowler lost two
front teeth and spent the next five minutes flat on his back,
his thoughts a million miles from the cricket field. Eventually
John Willy was given out for 'ungentlemanly conduct' and the
fast bowler taken to the local infirmary for a check up. Soon
after John Willy was called before the disciplinary committee
and severely reprimanded.

The following Christmas he found his cap on the snowman
and being the sort of man who could read the signs better than
most he retired. We gave him a presentation dinner the following season and the chairman of the club, while handing him
a chromium plated cake stand, described him as a 'great
captain and a gentleman'. We were not sure how John Willy
would react to being called a 'gentleman', but he took it very
well. Nor did he disagree with being called a 'great captain'.
What he said was, 'Me and D. R. Jardine played it t'same
way.' So far as I know Douglas Jardine never chinned a fast
bowler, but we all knew what John Willy meant.

9 Webb

When I was five years old, the old man bought me a cricket bat. The blade was creamy, the handle red, and it was the best bat I ever possessed.

I picked it up for the first time and stood in the approved position, left shoulder pointing down the wicket, left toe cocked in honour of George Roberts, the local big hitter, who at the time I considered the best batsman in the world. My old man patiently took the bat from me, turned me so my right shoulder pointed down the wicket and nodded in satisfaction. Thus, a left-handed bat was created against nature's whims.

I didn't question the move at the time, but later the old man explained everything. 'No bowler likes left-handers lad. Remember that and think on that you've got a head start.' As a bowler himself he reckoned he knew what he was talking about. He hated bowling at 'caggy handers.'

When he finished bowling and became captain of our second team he worked on the simple philosophy that the more left-handed batsmen he could discover or invent the better our chances of victory. He proved his point by winning the championship with a team which included nine left-handed bats, four natural, five manufactured. He took great delight in the freakish nature of his team and loved observing the mounting incredulity of his opponents as left-handed bat followed left-handed bat to the wicket. After the first half dozen, the opposing captain would often turn to the old man, lurking on the boundary edge, and say, 'Ayup skipper. 'Ow many more bloody caggy 'anders siree?'

Whenever I think about that team I always begin wondering about the number of people who affect our outlook and attitudes on sport. I am cricket mad because I caught the complaint from my old man, but even that condition might have been cured had it not been for someone else. He was the sports master at the local grammar school, a large craggy man who had been good enough to play both football and cricket at professional level.

The first time I came across him he was bowling at the nets at we youngsters who were hoping to make the under-14 team. His first ball to me was a little short of a length and being young and full of madness I went for a hook and missed by a mile. It didn't seem very important to me and I was therefore a little taken aback on returning the ball to see the master, hands on hips, staring at the sky. He remained like that for some time, lips moving silently, and then he looked at me.

'What was that?' he asked.

'A hook sir,' I said. 'Hook?' he said shaking his head. 'A hook? At your age you shouldn't even know what it means.'

It was the best possible introduction to the man who for the next four years was to coach me in the game. He taught in the great Yorkshire tradition, concentrating solely on backward and forward defensive play. Any strokes we played that required the bat moving from the perpendicular were better done when he wasn't looking. I once played a late cut for four in a school game when I thought he was in bed with 'flu and as my eyes proudly followed the ball to the boundary, I saw him standing there sadly shaking his head at the horror of it all.

I once heard him admonish another master whom he caught demonstrating the square cut to a young player: 'Be it on your own head.'

For all he was a puritan about cricket he was a marvellous coach. He turned out a succession of young cricketers who were so well versed in the rudiments of the game that they found the transition from schoolboy cricket to the leagues fairly painless.

His one blind spot was a total inability to appreciate the odd exceptional talent that came his way. Everyone had to conform to his basic principles no matter how rich their natural gifts. At the time I was at school we had in our team a batsman called Hector of remarkable ability.

Hector, who was shaped like a junior Colin Milburn, had no time for acquiring defensive techniques. He approached each ball as if it was the last he would ever receive on this earth, and that being the case, he was going to try to split it in two. For a schoolboy he was an exceptional striker of the ball, blessed with a powerful physique, a quick eye and a sure sense of timing. He played some fine innings for the school teams, but no matter how brilliantly he played, he never pleased the sports master.

'Defence, Hector lad, defence,' the sports master would say, and Hector would put one foot down the track and blast the ball straight for six and the sports master would look sorrowful. The high point of their relationship occurred in a masters versus boys game in which the sports master opened the bowling and Hector opened the batting. He played one of his best innings that day, thrashing the bowling, particularly the sports master's, without mercy.

The master kept the ball up as he always taught us to do, and Hector kept thumping away. He had scored about 86 in 30 minutes when he hit over one of the sports master's deliveries and was bowled. As he walked towards the pavilion the sports master said triumphantly: 'I warned you Hector lad, that's what fancy play gets you.'

He was the only man on the field, or off it, who remained convinced that Hector had failed. It would have pleased him more if Hector had observed the rules that bound us lesser players and carried his bat for a dour thirty.

But for all that, he was a good man who taught a lot of boys a proper respect for the most difficult and beautiful of games.

When I saw him last, he looked old and ill and said he had retired as a sports master. He told me he watched the school team occasionally but had invariably been disappointed by what he saw. 'Too much flashing about, not enough straight bat,' he said.

He stood up to demonstrate his point. 'Cricket is about this . . .' He played forward with an imaginary bat. 'And this . . .' He played back. 'And not this . . .' And he executed what I can only describe as a derogatory late cut.

His name was Webb Swift and I heard recently that he had died. The chances are you've never heard of him. He wasn't a famous man, just important to a lot of people like me who learnt to love cricket at his knee, and whenever I think about people who have affected my life, I remember him.

10 Anything goes

To have played cricket and never taken part in a knock-out competition is like joining the Army and never hearing a shot fired in anger. Knock-out cricket is designed to bring the worst out of players and spectators alike. It gives off that most delicious of cricket perfumes: the heady whiff of crushed grass and skullduggery.

My old man adored knock-out cricket. Being the sort of player who could turn a gentle game of beach cricket into something resembling the landing at Iwo Jima he relished the tense and often violent atmosphere of knock-out cricket. Much of the excitement at these games comes from the spectators whose normal ration of pride in the local team is supplemented by the fact that they have ten bob on the game with the local bookie.

My old man tells a lovely story of the time he played his first knock-out game. His father was a big betting man and was well pleased when the opposition was bowled out for 42.

It seemed a walkover for my old man's team, so much so that when he went to look at the batting order the skipper had only put down four names and said to my dad: 'Off tha' goes Sammy. We shan't need thee.'

Fortunately he stuck around long enough to see his team collapse to the extent that when he went out to bat at No. 11 his side were 20 for 9 wickets and needed 23 to win. As he went down the pavilion steps he was the object of much excellent advice from the betting fraternity, none more pithy than that offered by his father, who said, 'If tha' gets out before we've beaten them I'll thump thee ear'ole.'

Basing his innings on this sound advice my old man managed to keep his end up while the batsman at the other end scored the runs to win the game.

The rejoicing was great and my old man was later downing a hero's pint in a nearby hostelry when he was approached by a local who said:

'Spending thi' collection money then, Sammy?'

'What collection?' said my old man.

'That what thi' father organised after tha'd won t'game for us. Collected about five quid on thi' behalf.'

Father swallowed his pint and dashed to the ground where he met his old man lurching gently away from the bar.

'Where's my collection then?' he said.

'Supped it' said his old man, burbing loudly.

It would be wrong to assume however that knock-out cricket only affects the spectators. It is beautifully designed to corrupt everyone who comes in contact with it.

In the knock-out cricket I used to play in, the right to cheat your way to victory was not written in the laws but it was certainly branded deep into the soul of every player. The rules allowed each team to play two professionals which meant that every team went to extra-ordinary lengths to play as many professionals as they could without their opponents finding out. As local professionals were well known the illegal ones had to be imported from nearby towns. When I played in these games they used to give the illicit professionals false names.

All this changed the year that the winning team was found to comprise of two Browns, four Smiths and five Jones. A subsequent inquiry revealed they were all professionals from the Lancashire League with names like Leatherbarrow and Strongitharm. After that the rules were changed and the teams had to declare the correct names of their players before the competition started. But there were ways round that. Once we arrived to play a team in the semi-final and the opposing captain popped into our dressing-room just before the game started to say he was a man short. 'Can I borrow a substitute, Fred,' he asked our skipper. 'No,' he replied, helpfully.

The opposing skipper then asked if he could pick a substitute from the spectators, and Fred agreed only if he had the right to veto. They set off round the ground together looking for likely prospects. Every time the opposing captain indicated a husky young lad Fred, who was enjoying himself immensely, would shake his head and point to an old man in a wheel chair. They had made a complete circuit of the ground and reached the pavilion again when the opposing captain pointed to a hunched, wizened figure sitting on the grass. An Indian wearing a bus conductor's uniform. Our captain thought this was a huge joke.

'They've got Gunga Din playing for them,' he told us. Someone reminded him cautiously that Indians could play cricket. 'But he's a bus conductor not Ranjitsinhji,' he replied. He received the first inkling of the way in which he had been deceived when we batted. After a couple of overs the little Indian was asked to bowl which was a bit strange considering they had found him on the ground only ten minutes earlier. We had our suspicions confirmed in the Indian's first over which contained five leg breaks and one googly of a quality normally reserved for Test batsmen. From that moment we knew our captain had been tricked and that we were doomed. The Indian took eight wickets for less than 20 and we lost the match.

Our skipper was fit for nothing after the game. He wasn't angry, just disappointed that he had not been the first to invent such a stunning piece of twisting. He just sat in the bar downing pints of bitter and staring moodily at the floor. But his worst moment was yet to come. The little Indian, back in his bus conductor's uniform, was sitting across the room with the winning team when someone asked him, just to rub it in, who was the best batsman he had bowled to. Everyone on our side stopped talking and listened because we still didn't know who or what he was.

Our skipper burped wittily and said sarcastically, 'Bradman.'
'No,' said the Indian, 'I think Len Hutton was the best.'   It
was too much for the skipper. He gave all his gear away and
swore he would never play again. We never did find out who
that little Indian was.

What we did learn, however, those of us reared on knock-out
cricket was that while it is perfectly true that the game can
uplift the spirit and make men angels it can also stimulate the
darkest corners of a man's personality and turn him into a
criminal mastermind.

11 Brotherly love

I used to play cricket with a man called Billy Hopkinson who made Pancho Gonzales look like the best behaved athlete in the world. Whenever he was given out LBW his team-mates would evacuate the dressing-room taking all their gear with them before Billy returned to vent his rage on whatever he could put his hands on. The main sufferers were the unfortunate batsmen who were at the crease when Billy was given out.

All they could do was stand and watch as their gear came through the dressing-room window to be followed by Billy's gear, the wooden benches, the matting floor carpet and, on very bad days, the large brown teapot that the tea ladies borrowed from the Church Hall and which was only used for funerals and cricket matches.

As befitted a world class tantrum-thrower, Billy Hopkinson could produce an outburst at the correct tactical time. He was the best ooer and aaher I ever played with and also the best running commentator.

On arriving at the wicket the new batsman would find Billy staring thoughtfully at a spot just short of a length. 'Looks nasty to me that does,' he'd say, sometimes going on his hands and knees to calculate the size of an imaginary ridge.

'I've never fancied this wicket since our Albert got his nose broke. Made a right messit did. You could hear the crack a mile away. Off a slow bowler, too,' he would say while the batsman tried to look cool.

From that point on the batsman's survival depended on his ability to concentrate on a game while being subjected to a barrage of propaganda from Billy at first slip. Any ball that went past the bat would bring an anguished 'Ooooh' or Aaaaer' from Billy. It didn't matter if it was a yard outside the off stump, Billy reacted as if it had passed through the wickets.

Not surprisingly Billy wasn't the most popular cricketer in the district. There were many players who disliked having been bowled out while in the middle of an argument with Billy about whether or not the previous ball had shaved the wickets.

One player dismissed in such a manner decided on swift justice and instead of returning to the pavilion set off after Billy waving his bat like a club. But Billy was soon three fields away and he wisely took no further part in the game, spending the afternoon at home and sending his missus down to the ground for his kit.

I only saw him beaten at his own game once and that was by a dark, squat little man who answered everything Billy said about him with a tiny smile, a neat bow of the head and a 'Thank you very much.' Finally Billy could endure it no longer.

At the end of the over he confronted the batsman: 'Ayup mister. I've been talking to thee all afternoon and tha's said nowt. What's up?' The batsman looked at him, smiled, bowed and said: 'Thank you very much.' Billy turned in despair to the other batsman. 'What the bloody hell's up wi' thi' mate,' he said.

'Didn't tha' know Billy? He doesn't speak English. He's Polish,' the batsman said.

'Polish!' said Billy. 'Polish! What's a bloody Polisher doing playing cricket?'

He was silent for the rest of the afternoon, only occasionally muttering the odd obscenity about foreigners. It never occurred to him that there was something very odd about a Pole who spoke no English and yet played cricket well. He was too busy fuming to consider that he might have been conned by a superior foe.

None of us dare put the point to him and indeed we were glad we didn't for otherwise we should have missed those marvellous moments in subsequent matches when after giving a new batsman the ritual spiel he would look at him and say: 'I suppose tha' speaks English lad?'

Normally his tantrums were designed to win a cricket match but once he lost one with a display of temperament which was spectacular even by his own high standards.

An occasional member of the team was Billy's brother, the aforesaid Albert who was reputed to have had his nose broken by a slow bowler. Whatever brotherly love they might have had for one another they kept well hidden on the cricket field. Billy believed Albert was useless and Albert's opinion of Billy was unprintable. The more tense the game, the more bitter became the feeling between them.

Their loathing of one another boiled over in one game when Albert was bowling the final over against the last two batsmen of the opposing side who wanted four to win. The very last ball of the game was struck by the number eleven straight to brother Billy who dropped the catch. Albert stood, hands on hips, glowering at his errant brother. 'You great twerp,' he bellowed. Billy, by now purple with embarrassment at having dropped the catch and enraged by his brother, shouted back:

'Tha' don't deserve wickets bowling bloody long 'ops like that.'

'Don't make excuses. I could have copped that in mi' gob. Tha' couldn't catch pneumonia,' said Albert.

This proved too much for Billy. Picking up the ball he advanced on his brother. 'If tha' so good at catching let's see thi' stop this one,' he said. He was about four yards from Albert when he threw the ball with all his considerable power. Wisely Albert ducked and the ball went for four overthrows and we had lost the match.

Billy and Albert were still arguing as we went back to the dressing rooms. Later they went behind the pavilion for a fight and were still at it when we left the ground. They both retired soon after that and went to barrack Yorkshire sitting at opposite ends of Bramall Lane.

Some years later I was reminded of Billy when I was playing for Barnsley against a team which contained a character renowned for his tantrums and his gamesmanship. He was a quick bowler and particularly rough on young players. He was bowling against us in one match and doing well both as a talker and a bowler until our number five batsman came to the wicket.

He was a young spindly lad with National Health spectacles and a bat which seemed several sizes too large for him. As he took guard the fast bowler commenced the treatment. 'Sending in short-sighted dwarfs to play us now. Must be short of players,' he shouted to the wicket-keeper.

His first ball was a good one a shade short outside the off stump. The batsman went on the back foot, the bat flashed and the bowler was left speechless as the ball sped to the boundary. It was the shot of a class batsman. The bowler turned to me and said ruefully: 'Not bad, not bad. What's his name?'

'Boycott, Geoffrey Boycott,' I said.

BOOK 2 Second innings

Those who can't play write about it

12 Wilfred

Wilfred Rhodes is in his nineties and still a young man. It was
my grandfather who first told me about him. He once walked
the 30 miles to Bradford to see Rhodes play and he never
forgot it.

Rhodes didn't let him down: 'He took six or seven wickets
that day without breakin' sweat and I said to a bloke sitting
next to me: "How's tha' reckon he'll do in t'second innings?"
and he says, "T'same," and I said "How's tha' know?" and
he said "If Wilfred does thi' once he'll do thi' aggean. He's
spotted thi' weakness tha' sees and if he's done that tha'
bound to be Wilfred's next time round." And he was right
tha' knows. Next innings he did t'same. Ah, he was a good 'un
Wilfred. Tha' could walk 30 miles and reckon on him doing
summat.'

Throughout his career Wilfred Rhodes specialised in always
'doing summat.' When he retired from the game he had scored
39,802 runs and taken 4,187 wickets. Only 10 batsmen in the
history of the game have scored more runs and no bowler
has come within a thousand wickets of Rhodes. Only George
Hirst is within two of his 16 doubles of 1,000 runs and 100
wickets in the same season, only Tich Freeman within six of his
23 years of taking 100 wickets and no one else has ever twice
made over 2,000 runs in a season and three times taken over
200 wickets.

As Sir Neville Cardus wrote: 'The man's life and deeds take
the breath away.' His career began with him playing against
W. G. Grace in Victoria's reign and ended in the thirties when
he played against Bradman. He played first class cricket for
32 years surviving every changing fashion in the game, shrugg-
ing off every potential challenger to his crown. Even today, at
the age of 90, the crown is still his.

There are, I suppose, more stories about Rhodes than any
other cricketer. He has attracted many faithful chroniclers. My
favourite, because it reveals the rare respect which Rhodes
commanded from his fellow professionals, is told by Cardus.
To illustrate Rhodes' known mastery of exploiting sticky
wickets Sir Neville tells of Charles McGahey, the old Essex
player, going out to bat on a sunny day at Bramall Lane,
Sheffield. As McGahey walked out to face Rhodes and Yorkshire the weather changed. Looking over his shoulder at the
darkening sun McGahey said, 'Ullo! Caught, Tunnicliffe;
bowled Rhodes . . .0.' And so it was, both innings.

I never saw Wilfred Rhodes play cricket. He had been retired
seventeen years when I saw my first Yorkshire game but I
fancy I knew more about his deeds than I did of the other
players who took the field that summer's day in 1947. My
grandfather and my father had crammed my young head with
tales about him. I first saw him at the Scarborough festival.
Play had not started when he entered the ground. He was
blind and being led. As he walked by the crowd stood and
doffed their hats and said, 'Ayup, Wilfred lad' and he nodded
and said, 'Ayup.' I measured off my youth with visits to
Scarborough to see the festival and gaze in awe at Wilfred
Rhodes.

And later, much later, when my job gave me the excuse, I
dared to sit with him. He was listening to the cricket and
talking to Bob Appleyard. Jackie Hampshire was batting and
he struck a ball massively over the square leg boundary, his
bat making a sound like a hammer hitting an anvil. Wilfred
stopped his discourse. 'I'll bet that went some way,' he said.

Appleyard said: 'Six over square leg. Jackie was sweeping.' Wilfred said scornfully, 'Sweeping. That nivver was any sort of shot. Once I was listening to television and a cricketer was coaching youngsters how to sweep. I had to switch it off.'

I remembered that Rhodes, after retiring from the county game, had coached at Harrow and asked him if he enjoyed it. 'It was alright,' he said, 'but them young lads were over-coached when they came to me. Tha' could always tell what they'd do, allus forward, ever forward. I used to run up to bowl and not let go and theer they'd be on t'front foot, leg stretched down t'wicket. And I'd walk up to 'em and say, "Na' then lad wheers tha' going. Off for a walk perhaps".'

He shook his head sorrowfully, 'Tha' knows one thing I learned about cricket: tha' can't put in what God left out. Tha' sees two kind of cricketers, them that uses a bat as if they are shovelling muck and them that plays proper and like as not God showed both of them how to play.'

I remarked how strange it seemed that he, the quintessential Yorkshire professional, the man who 'laiked proper' and not

for fun, should teach cricket at one of the temples of the
amateur game.

'Lads were alright,' he said. 'I liked them, we got on well. It
was t'others, t'masters I couldn't get on with. They allus
thought they knew more than me. I told one of 'em one day
he'd been interferin' and I said "Tha' can't know more about
this game than me tha' knows" and he said, "Why not?"
and I said, "Because if th'did tha'd be playing for England and
I'd be doing thy job teaching Greek".'

Listening to Rhodes one is transported to a world where
cricketers wore sidewhiskers and starched the cuffs of their
shirts; a game of gentlemen and players, separate entrances,
attitudes as different as night and day. Because his mind sees
them clearly he introduces you to Trumper and Ranji and
Grace and Gregory and Armstrong and Plum Warner. He
can conjure up cricket in Victorian England, in the first world
war, through the depression years to the 'Golden Thirties'.
He is a walking history of the game, blessed with a fabulous
memory and the unequivocal attitude of one who is certain
of what he says for the simple reason that he was there when it
happened. When Wilfred Rhodes tells you that Bradman was
the best bat that ever lived and that S. F. Barnes was the best
bowler only the foolish would dare argue.

'It's a thinking game is cricket. If tha' doesn't use thi' brains
tha' might as well give up. When I took up batting serious
and opened wi' Jack Hobbs in Australia, a lot said I couldn't
bat. But I thought about it and decided that t'best way to go
about t'job in Australia was to play forward. In that trip I
made one or two (including a record opening partnership
of 323 with Hobbs which still stands) and one day I'm going
on t'tram to t'ground and Duff t'Australian cricketer sits
next to me and starts chatting. He said "Tha' knows tha'
baffles me Wilfred," and I said "How come?" and he says,
"Well tha's got all these runs on this tour and yet tha' can't
bat. Tha's only got one shot." And I said "Ay, and that's all
I need out here." Same with bowling, too, although you could
say I was more gifted than most at it. But I still used to think

'em out. Batsmen used to say about me that I could drop a ball on a sixpence. Now that's impossible, no one can do that. I could probably hit a newspaper, spread out at that. But point is they used to think I could hit a sixpence and I used to let 'em keep on thinking and that way they were mine.'

During our talk he riffled through the years, illuminating forgotten summers with his yarns, breathing life into cricketers long dead. About M. A. Noble, the great Australian all-rounder who captained his country at the turn of the century, he said: 'That Noble was a good 'un. Used to bowl his quicker one with his fingers straight up t'seam. He nivver got me.' On Geoffrey Boycott, who played for England 70 years later: 'I said to him one day, "Does tha' cut?" And he said, "A bit" and I said "Remember not to do it until May's finished".'

He lives at present with his daughter Muriel and her husband Tom near Bournemouth. He still enjoys good health, takes a daily walk and listens to the radio. During the cricket season he keeps in touch with the game by occasional trips to Lords where he meets old friends eager for a yarn. His encyclopaedic mind is fed daily by fresh facts on cricket read to him from the papers by his daughter and son-in-law.

He doesn't miss a trick. I once wrote a story for the *Sunday Times* about an incident concerning W. G. Grace. During a Gentlemen versus Players fixture at Lords Schofield Haigh the Yorkshire player asked the good doctor's permission to leave the field early on the last afternoon so that he might journey back to Yorkshire. Permission was granted. On that last afternoon as the time for Haigh's departure and Grace's century drew nigh Grace hit an easy catch toward Haigh. As Haigh awaited the ball the Doctor shouted: 'Take the catch and you miss the train.' Not being daft Haigh missed the catch and in consequence was home in Yorkshire when he wanted to be.

Shortly after writing the story I received a letter. It simply said: 'That story you told about Schofield Haigh was true. I know because I was the bowler.' It was signed: Wilfred Rhodes. I still have it. I wouldn't swop it for a gold pig.

It's not everyone who gets a letter from the Gods.

13 Making a comeback

It has always been a golden rule of mine that critics should never be seen in public with their trousers down, if you know what I mean. The one certain way to end up in this particular predicament is for the critic to delude himself into believing that he can improve on the efforts of those he is paid to criticise. Being a foolish fellow and a bit of a dreamer, too, I once broke my golden rule by becoming a Yorkshire player. The occasion was a six-a-side tournament in aid of the admirable Jimmy Binks during his benefit year. The Yorkshire side was: Binks, Wilson, Nicholson, Hampshire, Hutton and Parkinson.

I ought to have known better. It's not as if I am without first hand experience of these things. I once played in a charity game with my dear friend Bill Grundy, whose television performances in Granadaland had won him a following which was sharply divided between those who thought he was the best thing since Ed Murrow, and those who nightly invoked God to strike him down. The fast bowler facing him on this occasion belonged to the latter school of thought and, no doubt impatient with God's reluctance to heed his prayers, decided to do the job himself. Over after over he hurled down a fearsome mixture of bouncers and beamers, many of which found the target and thudded into the flesh of my friend and colleague making a noise like a large door slamming. As I

I like thy overcoat

stood there watching him absorb punishment, just because the bowler didn't like him on the telly, I was filled with admiration at his brave refusal to give an inch. He just stood there and took it. Later in the pavilion when we were counting his bruises, I complimented him on his guts.

'You've got to be joking,' he said.

'But you were marvellous. You just stood there and let him hit you,' I said.

'Look, I'll let you into a little secret. The only reason I didn't move was because I couldn't see the damn ball. I could hear it coming, I could feel it hit me but I'll be damned if I could see it,' he said.

Given a lesson like that you would have thought that I would have resisted the temptation to turn out for Yorkshire in similar circumstances. But no. Out of practice and condition as I was, I rejected commonsense in favour of the vain notion that I might enjoy an afternoon as a Yorkshire cricketer.

So it was, I trooped onto the field wearing a Yorkshire sweater, kindly loaned to me by Peter Stringer, the fast bowler, who unfortunately happens to be a giant. The sweater fell somewhere around my knees and as I walked down the pavilion steps someone said, 'I like thi' overcoat.' I ignored him. By that time I was far too gone on my fantasy to care. I was preoccupied with deciding whether or not to be F. S. Parkinson, the demon bowler taking the field, needing one wicket for his thousand in first-class cricket, or D. C. S. Parkinson going out in a fading light with a bloodied bandage round my head to fight off Lindwall and Miller.

As I took my position at long-off, I studied my team mates, calculating how I might compare in the field with them. Four of them offered me no hope. There was Binks, as immaculate and sure as ever behind the stumps, Don Wilson, one of the best fielders in Christendom, Jack Hampshire, burly and safe with a right arm like a blacksmith's, and Richard Hutton who is useful. Only the last member of our team, Tony Nicholson, offered me any consolation.

Now Nicholson is a fine bowler and an engaging man, but not even his best friend would describe him as the most nimble fielder in the world. I decided that should I make a hash of things in the field, I would look to Nicholson for sympathy and understanding. Which only goes to show how naive I am.

The first time I fielded the ball and threw in, Jimmy Binks averted the horror of six overthrows by a miraculous feat of aerobatics. I looked toward Nicholson, 'Tha' throws like a big soft lass,' he said, without malice. I was still smarting under this when I set off in long and vain pursuit of a cover drive struck off Nicholson. I hit the boards about the same time as the ball, but whereas the ball stopped on the field of play, I tripped and fell down the embarkment. When I returned to the field slightly bruised but content that I had given of my best, it was to be greeted by Nicholson with: 'It's a good job it went for four.' And when I inquired why, he replied, 'Because way thar throws they'd have run six by t'time Binksy got ball.'

By now I was completely deflated and beginning to realise my mistake. But the worst was yet to come. Again Nicholson was bowling when I attempted to field a ball which popped out of my palsied hands. By the time I had recovered it and returned it to Jimmy Binks, the batsmen had run two. Nicholson's revenge was swift and terrible. He bellowed across the field, 'Parky, tha'rt fielding like a big twassock.'

Now it may be that like me you have not come across the word 'twassock' before. But to hear Tony Nicholson deliver it last week was to understand perfectly what it means. Even my only moment of triumph on that horrendous afternoon, was curdled by the observations of a man I had once thought of as my friend. After taking a running catch on the boundary, much to the surprise of myself and my colleagues, I was basking in the startled applause when Nicholson approached me. 'That was a good catch,' he said. 'Thank you kind sir,' I said. 'What's tha' been taking,' he asked. I said I didn't understand. 'Well t'way tha' ran and copped that ball just now I thought tha' must be taking dope,' he said.

Not a shred of my original, beautiful fantasy remained as I limped from the field. As I walked towards the pavilion, a young lad asked me for my autograph. I felt pleased that at least one youngster had been persuaded by my performance, that underneath the outsize sweater there lurked a Yorkshire cricketer. He handed me his books open at a section marked 'Yorkshire Team'. As I prepared to sign he said, 'Not there mister' and opened the book at the back to a section marked— 'Miscellaneous'. I put my name alongside the signature of someone called Herbert Delaney, and the inky paw mark of 'Rover, the talking dog'.

My only consolation from that sorry afternoon was the knowledge that critics are not the only people who indulge their fantasies. Sometimes it happens to sportsmen. The best example I know concerns a Yorkshire cricketer who was once persuaded to make a guest appearance with a repertory company in his home town.

It was a tiny part requiring him to walk through the french windows immaculate in white flannels, striped blazer and straw boater and say to the assembled company: 'Prudence and I wonder if any of you would care to join us for a spot of tennis.' During rehearsals the producer, with much skill and patience, persuaded a reasonable performance out of the cricketer, even managing to smooth out his thick Yorkshire accent. On the opening night our hero swept through the french windows, handsome and athletic, looked round the stage and forgot his lines. As he stood there, desperately trying to remember, he caught sight of the tennis racket in his hand and blurted out: 'Does any of your lot laik tennis?'

14 Those who stand and serve

I remember my first umpire well. His name was Jim Smith and he always took his teeth out before a game. I never discovered why but I always supposed it was a safety precaution due to the state of our wickets and the ferocity of our cricket.

He was a marvellous man, tall and dignified even without his teeth, with an infallible technique for puncturing swollen heads. I remember as a youngster playing well and scoring fifty or so in a game he was umpiring. I carried my bat and as I came off the field, triumphant, imagining myself to be an unbelievable mixture of Bradman and Hutton, he joined me at my shoulder. As we walked in together, I looked towards him anticipating a word of praise. He glanced sidelong at me and out of the corner of his mouth said: 'Does tha' want some advice, lad?'

I said I did.

'Well get thi' bloody hair cut,' he said.

Two matches later he gave me out lbw and as I walked sullenly past him he said, out of the same corner of his toothless mouth:

'If tha'd get thi' bloody hair cut tha'd stop them balls wi' thi' bat.'

Jim Smith was my introduction to that delightful body of men: the cricket umpire. I can think of no other group that does so much for so little. By comparison the soccer referee is a pampered ninny, and the fact that cricket has survived this far without requiring the umpires to take the field carrying truncheons says much for their character. The secret of course lies in their humour. There are few funny stories about soccer or Rugby referees and anyone who tells me a funny about a tennis umpire will receive a gold plated pig by return of post. But there is a Bumper Fun Book of Funny Umpire stories.

Many of them concern Alec Skelding. My favourite Skelding story concerns the aggrieved batsman who, on being given out lbw, addressed Skelding thus:

'Where's your white stick umpire?'

'Left it at home,' said Alec.

'What about your guide dog,' said the batsman.

'Got rid of it for yappin' same as I'm getting rid of you,' replied Skelding.

Joe Hayes never rose to Skelding's heights in cricket but in the local league I played in as a youth he was just as big a legend. Those who knew Joe well, always appealed for everything as opening time approached because Joe had a job as a waiter in a local boozer and had to be on duty at 6 p.m. It was his proud boast that he had never been late at the boozer for 20 years and could produce several hundred cursing batsmen to bear him witness. His other quirk was a dislike of loud appealing. He himself rarely raised his voice above a murmur and his face creased in pain and disgust whenever a bowler bellowed in his earhole.

We had in our team at the time the best appealer of all time. His voice rattled windows several miles away and set dogs to whimpering. This particular game his raucous appeals eventually got on Joe's nerves. After one particularly loud one Joe could stand it no longer.

'Owz that,' bellowed the bowler.

'Not out,' Joe bellowed back in an even louder voice. The bowler stood amazed that Joe should raise his voice.

'I'm only bloody askin' thi',' he said in a pained tone.

'Ay and I'm only bloody tellin' thi',' shouted Joe.

All of which leads to Cec Pepper who as a player in the Lancashire League was renowned as much for his verbal battles with umpires as he was for his cricketing prowess.

Pepper was the scourge of Lancashire League umpires, blasting the meek with his belligerent appealing, making the lay preachers blush with his vivid language. The umpire who faced up to him had to be a special kind of human being and George Long was such a man.

George was standing one day at the end where Pepper was bowling, when Pepper made one of his raucous Australian appeals for lbw, which was answered by a quiet 'Not out.' Whereupon Pepper gave vent to a histrionic stream of invective, throwing in all the stock-in-trade props—spectacles, white stick, guide dog, illegitimacy, bloody-minded Englishness, and four-letter words: all of which George completely ignored.

The same thing happened after the next ball and yet again the following one, after which George called 'Over' and walked to his square leg position, followed by Pepper—obviously disturbed by the lack of reaction from the umpire.

'I suppose you're going to report all this bad language to the League?' said Pepper.

'No' replied George. 'Ah likes a chap as speaks his mind.' Pepper was obviously delighted.

'So do I,' he said smiling, 'and I must say it's a refreshing change to meet an umpire like you. I'm glad that we understand each other.'

'Aye,' said George.

The first ball of the next over again hit the batsman's pad, whereupon Cec whirled round to George, arms outstretched and did his usual Red Indian war whoop. His 'Howzat' was heard all round the ground.

'Not out, you fat Australian bastard,' said George quietly.

15 Keep the home fires burning

*Albert Crump, 32, a stevedore, of Wapping, was reunited yes-
terday with his wife and children after an absence of five years.
Mr. Crump, who left home in 1962 to play cricket for his local
team, told our reporter: 'After the game I missed the last bus
home and I decided to walk it. I just got lost.' Mrs. Ruby
Crump said: 'My Albert never had a sense of direction.'*
  News Item.

The problem of getting home from cricket matches is one
which faces every sportslover once he has allowed a woman to
come between himself and the game he loves.

Every cricketer who has been faced with the decision of
oiling his bat or taking his wife to the boozer will understand
what I mean. The real problem is that women are incapable of
understanding that cricket is not the sort of game which, if it
ends at 6.30 means that husband will be home with his feet up
at seven.

So long as women refuse to face up to this so long will players
like Mr. Albert Crump go to extraordinary lengths to have their
way. I once played in a team at Hull and having arrived home
at about 9.30 was amazed to receive a phone call from our fast
bowler who was still in that noble city.

'It's the wife. She'll bloody skin me when I get home,' he
said, explaining the call.

I asked what on earth I could do.

'Well you could ring her or something,' he said.

'But what would I say?'

'I've thought about that. Tell her I've gone somewhere.'

'But where?' I asked.

'Copenhagen,' he said.

Now I have had some curious propositions put to me in my short life, but this one topped the lot. 'Look,' I said. 'Kindly explain to me how you, who have just played cricket in Hull, manage to get to Copenhagen.'

'Simple. Tell the wife I had a message from the office delivered at the ground and that I had to take off.'

Eventually I agreed to ring his wife. I tried to make the message sound as plausible as possible. She listened in silence and then said: 'If you see him when he gets back tell him I had a message too and that I've gone to live with our Hilda in Sheffield . . . for good.'

I first came face to face with cricket as a breaker-of-marriages when I was a youth and playing in a team with a character called Sammy. After my first game he said to me: 'Na' then, tha'rt too young to go boozin' so what tha' can do is tek mi cricket bag to our house. Na' when tha' gets theer dooant knock on t'door or else tha'll alert t'old lass. Just sling t'bag in t'garden and run off.'

When I arrived at his house his wife was standing by the gate arms folded, very tight lipped.

'Tha's come to chuck t'bag in t'yard,' she said. I nodded.

'Wheer is he then?' she asked.

I started to explain but she interrupted 'Suppin' I suppose,' she said and went indoors. I slung the bag and left.

The next week I asked one of my team mates about Sammy and the wife. He explained that there had been open warfare between the two for many years about the amount of time Sammy spent away from home in the cricket season. Once, it was rumoured, Sammy's wife had threatened to come to the game with him, and was only prevented from doing so by Sammy fastening her by her pinafore in the rollers of one of those big old-fashioned mangles and taking the handle out so that she couldn't free herself.

But she had not surrendered the fight and eventually they had arrived at a compromise. Every Saturday someone would sling Sammy's bag in the backyard. If, when he returned, the bag had been taken inside by his wife, Sammy would know that all was forgiven and he could share the marital couch. If however the bag lay where it had been hurled, he would know that the wife was sulking and would lurch his way to the spare bed. The system seemed to work, its great advantage being it avoided those unseemly and noisy rows between man and wife that sometimes follow a day at the cricket.

In fact Sammy's old woman had no intention of giving in so easily and what appeared on the surface to be a civilised agreement between two grown people was in fact an elaborate booby trap designed by a woman scorned.

One Saturday after several week-ends in the spare bed, Sammy arrived home to find his bag had been taken inside. Quickened by the anticipation of the next few hours he galloped into his bedroom only to be felled by a fearsome blow from his own willow. When he awoke it was to discover that his wife had run off with the local bookie, but not before she had repaid Sammy for all the awful hours she endured as a cricket widow.

16 Comic cricket

In recent years my appearances on the field to play have been limited and greeted by much hilarity. Not that I cut a comical figure on the field, quite the reverse for I have been referred to as the 'Ted Dexter of Barnsley.' It is simply that the cricket I have been involved in has been for charity and of a type known as 'Comic Cricket.'

To play comic cricket one must be prepared to swallow one's pride in more ways than one. For instance, one must allow oneself to be bowled out by some long-haired, twittish pop star, or serve up leg side full tosses so that some TV personality might score a few runs. Then there is the matter of appearance. I'm a romantic about cricket. I love the sight of white figures flitting o'er the greensward and therefore object when this vision is defiled by some person of unspecified sex taking the field in jockey cap, kaftan and rope sandals.

Professional cricketers are funny about cricket. Some, like Geoffrey Boycott, are unable to play the game other than seriously. I remember once organising a comic cricket team and persuading Geoffrey to play. He put his head down as only he knows how and scored a marvellous century. But by doing so he split the game in two because while bowling at him the opposition played like demons, while at the other end the rest of us enjoyed the normal fruits of comic cricket such as donkey drops and catches missed on purpose. The one

Tha' looks like nowt on bloody earth

exception was a disc jocky who went in to join Boycott and was mortified when the first ball he received whistled through his hair. Quickly assessing the situation he walked down the wicket and addressed the bowler thus:

'Take a good look at me my man,' he said.

The fast bowler, brow thunderous after two hours of trying to penetrate Boycott's defence, looked at him. The disc jockey was attired according to the rules of comic cricket in that he was wearing canvas boots, Bermuda beach shorts, a psychedelic shirt, a necklace of worry beads and a tin helmet. The bowler looked at him for a long time.

'Do I look like a bloody cricketer?' said the disc jockey.

'Tha' looks like now't on bloody earth,' said the bowler. Then he thought a bit and said: 'And I'll tell thi' what, after t'next ball tha'll look even bloody funnier because I'm going to knock thi' bloody head off.'

Whereupon the disc jockey pleaded a prior engagement and left the field.

Umpires too have to be prepared to alter their ways if they wish to participate in comic cricket. For instance there are no LBW's in comic cricket and no one is given out before he has scored. Ensuring that these principles are firmly adhered to can put the umpire under severe strain.

In one game I organized, the beneficiary, a well known County and England player, had his stumps reduced to matchsticks by the first ball delivered to him by a young pace man eager to impress. The umpire, himself an old player, stood helpless as the beneficiary stormed from the field. However, a debate in our dressing room led to a compromise solution whereby, as we were one man short, the beneficiary was allowed to bat again. He went in at number six and we settled back to watch him wreak his revenge on the young upstart who had humiliated him. The first ball was of gentle pace outside the off stump. The beneficiary, too anxious to restore his name, flashed at it and snicked a catch to the wicket-keeper. The 'keeper caught the ball in a shamefaced sort of way, the fielders stared at the grass, when suddenly there was a lone cry of 'Owz that' from the umpire, who in the excitement of the moment had forgotten he was no longer a player. He stood there arms raised aloft until realisation of what he had done stained his face crimson. He lowered his arms and as he did said loudly: 'Not out, you daft old sod.'

The beneficiary then proceeded to score the 50 the crowd had come to see.

The most successful umpires in comic cricket are assuredly those who enter most willingly into the spirit of the occasion. The best two we ever had were certainly my old man and Bill Grundy's dad. Apart from their presence ensuring that Bill and myself were worth 50 apiece any time we played they were wholehearted devotees of comic cricket, particularly when it came to participating in the important ritual known as 'the pause for drinks.' This is the normal drinks interval which occurs infrequently in county cricket on hot days.

Our intervals were different in three important respects: (a) it didn't matter what the weather was like; (b) there were six drink intervals in every hour; (c) only alcohol was served. In a particularly gruelling session in the field, it was possible to get a little merry and there was the splendid occasion when after participating in the drinks ritual, the respective heads of the House of Grundy and the House of Parkinson called two armchairs on to the field and conducted their business in the most gentlemanly fashion, one sitting behind the stumps and one reclining at square leg.

But the truly marvellous thing about comic cricket is that it does wonders for the ego. If like myself you have let your game go to pot, what could be better than to play comic cricket and be guaranteed a few runs? Cricket without humiliation. A self-deception? Well I know that and so do you but what about in 20 years' time when someone finds a scorebook which says: M. Parkinson c. Boycott, bowled Trueman 57.

They're going to think I must have been pretty hot stuff. They're not going to know that Fred was bowling left-handed, they were using a tennis ball, and my old man was umpiring.

17 The problems of parenthood (Part 1)

The good thing about having an imagination as vivid as mine is that one can conjure magic out of the most ordinary circumstances.

For instance, I am one of the growing band of Britons that has a patio where his back garden ought to be. It is a paved square of land so tiny that on sunny days we have to take turns to sit on it. Nonetheless it was on this concrete postage stamp that one of cricket's great innings was played last week.

England were in dire trouble when I went to the wicket. They needed 400 to win on the last day and had already lost four wickets for 10 runs when I joined Boycott at the wicket. Together we batted through the long afternoon until at five minutes to six I straight-drove Sobers into the pavilion for six to bring my own score to 250 and victory for my country. I was nonchalantly waving away the encroaching hordes of delirious spectators when I was brought down to earth by my eldest son, Andrew.

'That is the fourth ball you have hit into next door's garden,' he said.

And there I stood, stripped of my fantasy, standing on my tiny patio gripping my son's cricket bat.

I said to Andrew: 'That was as fine a straight drive as you

will ever see, my son. What is more it has won the game for England.'

He gave me that pitying look of his and said: 'That is the fourth time you have hit the ball into the neighbour's garden. After the third time we made a rule: in a garden out. You are out.'

Sullenly I handed him the bat.

'Cheats never beat,' I said.

He shook his head sadly.

'It is your turn to fetch the ball,' he said.

I peered over the garden wall and came nose to snout with a large and fearsome dog who had the ball in his mouth. Now some of my best friends are dogs but I have never recovered from the fact that I was once bitten by one trying to recover a cricket ball in similar circumstances. The fact that the dog was the only Chow in Barnsley and District in no way lessened the pain nor prevented me from acquiring an acute dislike of approaching dogs with cricket balls where their teeth ought to be.

The dog and I faced each other for a while. I wondered whether I should send Andrew over the top but decided against it. So I called the whole thing off. 'Dog stops play,' I said.

'Always the same when It's my turn to bat,' said Andrew, and went off to find his roller skates. Left alone I considered my innings. I couldn't explain to Andrew that there was purpose in my fantasy, that I needed a long innings to put me in good heart for my real comeback three days hence when I would once more flit o'er the greensward for the *Sunday Times* against the *Sunday Express*. The innings on the patio was the final touch to a week of careful preparation. It was the only orgy I allowed myself that week. The rest had been an object lesson in calculated self-discipline.

For instance instead of parking the car next to the office I parked it at a garage three blocks away so that I might get a little morning exercise. I gave up cream with my strawberries and slept with the window open. After three days I felt considerably worse than my normal state which is awful, and it was then that I decided on my orgy of fantasy on the patio. I felt much better for it. It encouraged me to practise my forward defensive stroke in front of the bedroom mirror and I was only dissuaded from this pastime by our daily help who came in to make the beds and left hurriedly giving me a funny look.

With two days to go before my comeback I felt in reasonably good shape. Physically I might not be everyone's idea of a finely-tuned athlete but mentally I was as sharp as a newly-honed razor and eagerly anticipating a day of combat with the *Sunday Express*. I was even more reassured upon paying a visit to a well-known Fleet Street hostelry to find members of the opposition team training hard on the local rocket fuel. It was, therefore, feeling slightly superior and in good heart that I embarked on the final phase of my training schedule. This was to visit a London bookshop to buy a few cricket books in the hope that I might find some inspiration for my comeback. I browsed happily for a while and settled finally on Douglas Jardine's reports of the England/Australia series in 1934. Good steely stuff, I thought, to put me in fighting trim.

Carrying my purchase under my arm I strode with what I took to be athletic grace down the steps of the bookshop. Weren't these the pavilion steps at Lord's and wasn't I going forth to pulverise the *Sunday Express*? It was in this elated mood that I slipped and bounced in the most painful and inelegant fashion down the stairs to the floor below. I was attended to by two pretty young things in mini-skirts who treated me with that wary manner women reserve for strange drunks. I was about to explain that far from being inebriated I was an athlete making a comeback when I thought better of it and limped silently away.

Next morning, 24 hours from my comeback I woke up in considerable agony. My left elbow was a Technicoloured mess. I went to see my doctor.

'Athlete's get this sort of thing. Been playing tennis?' he said.

'No, I fell downstairs,' I said.

'Oh yes,' he said, and gave me a knowing wink.

'Look. I'm making a comeback. I am on the threshold of a great career in cricket. Heal me.'

'Not a chance for a week or two,' he said.

'I shall be brave about it,' I said through tight lips.

'Of course you could play one-handed,' the doctor said as I went through the door clutching my prescription.

That set me thinking. What a marvellous comeback it would be if with one hand I repulsed all that the *Sunday Express* could hurl at me. Parkinson in the line of Cowdrey and the Hon. Lionel Tennyson. I arrived home and immediately instructed Andrew to join me on the patio. We found another ball and I prepared for my one-handed innings that would save the day for England. I took guard and stuck my damaged arm inside my coat. The tension was terrific. The first ball delivered by a sulking Andrew bounced twice, hit a dog biscuit and shot under my bat to strike the plastic wash-basin we use as a wicket. There was nothing I could do. Andrew came towards me smirking in triumph.

'That was a sneaky thing to do to a cripple,' I said.

'It was my goggly,' he said.

'I am going in now to rest,' I said.

'What about my innings,' he asked.

'We will resume this game when I am back to peak health,' I said.

I went indoors to nurse my disenchantment. But for an insatiable literary appetite and an ancient dog biscuit I might have made my comeback and altered the entire course of my life. Thus are momentous events affected by the minutiae of living.

18 The problems of parenthood (Part 2)

I asked my eldest boy how he went on at school.

'We beat them 14-10,' he said.

'Look,' I said, 'I wasn't enquiring about football. I was enquiring about your general work. But since you mention it, why are you still playing Soccer at the end of April?'

'I don't understand.'

'Isn't it about time that you started playing cricket?'

'Why?'

I looked up from my task of putting bills into the lucky bag ready for my weekly draw.

'Because, dear child, the cricket season starts this week and for a Yorkshireman like yourself it should have begun in February.''

'Well, I prefer playing football.'

I stared at him in disbelief.

'Do you mean to say you don't like cricket?' I said.

'It's all right, but it's not as good as football,' he said.

I knew then it was time for a serious talk.

'Look, child, you must remember your background. Nine years ago, just before you were born, your mother was residing in Manchester. I was earning my bread in London and had arranged that you should be born free, gratis and for nothing

by courtesy of the National Health Service in a Manchester nursing home. Three days before the happy event I had a call from your grandfather informing me that at dead of night he had transported my sleeping wife over the Pennines and deposited her in a nursing home in Wakefield.'

'What's wrong with that?'

'Absolutely nothing, except that whereas you should have been a Lancastrian provided by courtesy of the Welfare State, you became a Yorkshireman brought into the world by private enterprise and at considerable expense to your poverty-stricken father.'

'I see. I'm sorry.'

'There is nothing to be sorry about. It wasn't your fault. But I don't think you appreciate what I am getting at. Why do you think your grandfather went to such inordinate lengths to have your born in Yorkshire?'

'I don't know.'

'Then let me tell you. You were kidnapped yet unborn and taken across the border to Yorkshire in order that you might be able to play for Yorkshire at cricket. The point being that only people born in Yorkshire can play cricket for Yorkshire.'

'Supposing I had been a girl?'

'That thought occurred to me too. Had you been a girl I would have sued your grandfather for the surgeon's fees.'

'Do many people go to Yorkshire to be born?'

'It is alleged that at the start of every cricket season the roads leading into the county are jammed with women being herded into Yorkshire by their husbands. This is what your grandfather says but then he tends to exaggerate.'

'Why weren't my brothers born in Yorkshire?'

'Ah, I'm glad you asked me that. Having once been the victim of your grandfather's guile, I made elaborate counterplans in the event of a further attempt to deny me the right to have my children born where I pleased and, moreover, on the National Health. That these plans were successful can be judged from the fact that both your brothers are today credits to the Welfare State. Moreover, one was born in Cheshire and the other in Berkshire. This added to the fact that we found our cat in Lancashire gives the family an international flavour which I find desirable.'

'Does that mean that you don't mind if my brothers and our cat don't play cricket?'

'Precisely. Your brothers will be encouraged to play the game but discouraged from playing the game at county level. I have other plans for them. Nicholas will be a brain surgeon and Michael will be a concert pianist. You are different. You must play cricket and will play for Yorkshire otherwise your grandfather will never speak to you again. Therefore it is important that you immediately put yourself to work toward that ambition, which is why you should be up in your room at this very moment practising forward and backward defensive shots in front of a full-length mirror.'

'You were born in Yorkshire weren't you?'

'Certainly,' I said.

'Then why didn't you play for Yorkshire at cricket?'

'Well the fact is I wasn't good enough.'

'Supposing I'm not good enough?'

'I shall cut you off without a penny.'

'Really?'

'Really.'

'Then I'd better start practising hadn't I?'

'You better had.'

'Very well but I'd still rather be Georgie Best,' he said, and went upstairs to practise his shots.

I returned to my task of putting my bills into the lucky bag pausing only now and then to contemplate the problems of parenthood.

19 Sand in my boots

There must be thousands of Englishmen who like me find their
holiday ruined if the beach is unsuitable for good cricket.

In the interest of these beach cricketers someone should
compile a guide to holiday places which offer the best facilities.
Such a guide should take into account size of beach, texture
of sand, natural hazards (such as an uncharted minefield), and
times of high and low tides. This last point is of great
importance.

Once at Scarborough playing for a Yorkshire eleven,
skippered inevitably by my old man, we were denied a well-
deserved victory over a Lancashire eleven, skippered by a coal
merchant from Aston-under-Lyne by a rapidly advancing tide
which caught deep square leg completely unawares. This
unfortunate fielder, thinking he was prepared for anything
with his trousers rolled above his knees and his cap on, was
knocked down from the rear by a large wave when going for a
critical catch and had to be rescued by the lifeguard. The game
was abandoned as a draw much to my old man's disgust.

From that day on my first task on arriving at the seaside
resort of our choice was to provide him with the week's
timetable of tides so that he could work out the day's play.

From my own experience I would unhesitatingly recommend
the East Coast resorts for lovers of beach cricket. Scarborough,
Filey and Bridlington are of Test Match standards and what

is more the people who holiday there are all likely to be keen devotees of the game. We only twice ventured away from the East Coast.

The first time we went to Blackpool, where, because of crowd conditions, we were forced to start our games at first light. Then we went to Ilfracombe, which the old man decided was unsuitable because the opposition was not up to scratch. He was put off that delightful resort the very first day we played there when the opposing wicket-keeper insisted on using his coat to stop the ball. My old man never played cricket on Famagusta beach, however, which was fortunate for his peace of mind.

I suppose it could be argued that I was expecting too much taking my cricket tackle to Cyprus, but that presupposes a lack of basic research on my part which is simply not true. I started at the tourist office in London. The girl told me all about the climate and then started on the beach. 'The finest in Cyprus if not the world,' she said. 'Any good for cricket?'

I said. 'I beg your pardon,' she said. 'Well, does it favour the batsman or the bowler?' I said. Eventually she understood the nature of my enquiry and assured me that everything would be to my satisfaction.

I should have known better than ask a woman about a matter of such importance. Also I should have read the signs better.

The first portent of disaster occurred at Nicosia Airport. The Customs Officer pointed at my cricket bag and inquired what it contained. 'Six stumps, two bats and several cricket balls of varying degrees of hardness,' I said.

'For what purpose?' he asked. 'For playing cricket of course,' I replied. 'In this heat?' he said. 'I have my pith helmet,' I responded amiably enough.

'The British,' he said, and shook his head.

When we arrived at the hotel we inspected the beach. I didn't like what I saw. The sand was too soft. Undeterred, we pitched stumps at eight the next morning and commenced play.

My first ball delivered from my full run (which is a slavish copy of Fred Trueman) pitched short and stopped dead. Close inspection revealed that it had buried itself six inches in the sand. We changed the leather ball for a tennis ball and I switched to bowling off-spinners with an action remarkably like Ray Illingworth's. The first ball pitched on a length and rolled to a stop six inches in front of the batsman. Being a Lancastrian and a scouser, which is even worse, he didn't do the decent thing but instead thumped me for six into the Mediterranean.

We tried a variety of balls but none of them worked on the sand which deadened any bounce. Eventually the beach boy, who had watched our performance with cynical amusement, came up with the solution. He produced a plastic football made in Italy and suggested we used that. I pointed out to him with great force that an English gentleman would never contemplate playing cricket with a football, whereupon he pointed out with equal fervour that it was the only practical solution. The scousers, who are not noted for their sensitivity in these matters, agreed with him. All I could do was retire in a huff, which I did.

I sent my old man a postcard explaining the situation and spent the rest of the holiday sulking in the sun. Any travel agent reading this piece who fancies taking my hard-earned money next year might note that I am not interested in the amount of sunshine available, nor in the cost of the local wine.

All I want, straight from the shoulder, is the state of the wicket.

20 Gentlemen of the press

Reporting cricket matches is not as simple as it seems. There are many occupational hazards any of which can deflect one's mind at the precise moment when history is being made. To start with there is the awful problem of trying to concentrate in a Press box while trying at the same time to forget that you are in one. For instance, the Press box at Leeds is designed specifically to attract every draught in Yorkshire. Even on a flawless summer day with the crowds in their shirtsleeves the sports writer must dress in long underwear, a sheepskin jacket, three sweaters, tightly laced knee boots and a balaclava if he is to feel at all comfortable. Rumours (as yet not denied) suggest that the Press box was designed by a firm specialising in the construction of wind tunnels.

It is possible as a cricket writer to experience climatic extremes in a few miles. Travel from Arctic Leeds to sunny Scarborough and you're in a different world. The Press box here is made of glass and is fondly referred to by the inmates as 'the sweat box.' Working here necessitates a complete change of uniform for the cricket writer. The experienced ones leave their winter clothes in the hotel and dress in canvas shoes, a sun weight, short sleeved towelling shirt with detachable hip tabs and tab-fastened sunglass pocket, and a pair of camel doeskin trousers slightly flared and with a Kampas stretch waistband. Anything more and he's over-dressed.

I elaborate only to prevent others experiencing the discomfort and embarrassment I had on my first visit to the ground. I arrived fully dressed for winter (as any sports writer would be who had just spent three days in August watching Lancashire at Old Trafford) and was greeted by slightly superior and knowing looks from my colleagues in the sweat box. After 10 minutes residence I had stripped off to my shirtsleeves and was wishing I hadn't got my long johns on.

The point is, of course, that with similar distractions in the Press box it is not surprising that details of play often pass unnoticed. You cannot, after all, be expected to be perceptive about a game when what you are really concerned about is the problem of removing your long underpants without being observed by either your colleagues or the spectators.

There are other reasons too why sports writers are caught napping. Often in a dull day's play with the deadline lurching toward you like a single-minded drunk at a party, the mind scrambles frantically for something interesting to write about. Often it comes up with something which seems good at the time but necessitates you taking your eye off the ball, so to speak. A simple story will illustrate.

I was once taking lunch in the pavilion of a Lancashire ground when the waitress, a cheery soul, said by way of making conversation:

'Yon Statham's badly.'

My antennae quivered. I remained calm.

'Ay, someone's put salt in t'sugar basin. Yon Statham's got a reet sweet tooth and he put fower spoonfuls in his tea. Well he supped it and his eyes pops out and he starts spluttering all over t'table. He thowt he's been poisoned I can tell you,' she said.

Well it wasn't that good a story after all. Not the sort to impress my sports editor. So I thanked her and forgot about it.

Back watching the cricket and remarking how sprightly Statham was in his first spell after lunch I said to my neighbour, 'very good for a man who was nearly poisoned.'

I ought to have known better. Quick as a flash he had me outside the Press box and pinned up against the wall. He worked for one of the smaller Sunday newspapers. I told him all.

'What a story. The headline must be "Sweet Tooth Gives Statham Bitter Taste of Success." Who did you get it from?' he asked.

'The waitress,' I said feebly.

He charged off in the direction of the dining room.

While he was away several interesting things happened on the field. Statham took a couple more wickets and someone was knocked out. When my friend returned I started telling him what he'd missed.

'Don't bother me with that stuff old man. It's a cover up. They've gagged her.'

'Who?'

'The waitress. Been told by the manager not to talk to the Press. Soon sorted him out though. Jumped-up kitchen hand. Told me to get lost. So I said to him, 'Don't start pulling rank with me little man. I've seen some service too y'know.' I told him we had a duty to publish the facts. Now let's see, how does the first paragraph go . . . "Brian Statham's sweet tooth gave him a bitter lesson today. But later it turned into the sweet smell of success." How's that then?'

'Exquisite,' I said.

'How many wickets has he got?'

'Six.'

'That's it then. Second paragraph . . . "Four spoonfuls of salt put by mistake in Brian Statham's lunchtime cuppa had the England bowler feeling ill. But after lunch it was the batsmen who felt sick as sweet tooth Statham took six wickets." Thanks old man. It's a great story.'

I didn't have the heart to tell him about the cricket. For all he knew they could have been throwing hand grenades at one another out in the middle.

He came back from phoning wreathed in smiles. 'Office love it. Just the job for my paper. No good for that rag of yours though. Must be tough writing for the qualities,' he said.

It is, by jove, it is. Tough for all of us who tread the bramble path of sports writing, which is why I thought it time that one of us should bare his breast and speak truthfully to the people who read the back pages first. When in future you read a report of a cricket match and wonder if the writer ever attended the game try to be charitable rather than abusive. Remember that the writer is one of that breed of men who suffer terrible privations to bring you the news. Sitting through a three day county game would test any normal man, but having to do so and write a clear report while sitting in a wind tunnel worrying about Brian Statham's guts requires a superhuman constitution worthy of your unstinted admiration.

21 Singing for my supper

I have been considering for some time whether or not to set a simple booby trap for the postman.

Nothing very clever. An electric letter box or a starving Alsatian might be the answer. It's not that I have anything against those brave boys in blue who defy the elements to bring me my post, it's what they carry that I object to.

Bills I can cope with; letters beginning 'Dear Big-Head . . .' I know how to handle. It's those invitations to speak at cricket dinners that make me jumpy.

Every year about now they start dropping like hand-grenades through my letter box, shattering my privacy, exploding my plans for a few evenings at home. They are well meant but based on three false assumptions: (a) that funny writers are funny speakers; (b) that everyone loves roast Norfolk turkey, chipolata sausages and game chips and (c) that I do not possess a wife with a suspicious mind.

In the main I find it hard to write a polite note of refusal without feeling a twinge of pity.

There are some invitations, of course, that one can turn down with a great amount of glee. These are the ones that start: 'Dear Sir, I have great pleasure in inviting you to speak at our annual dinner. Forgive us for the late invitation which was caused by the fact that Mr. E. W. Swanton is indisposed . . .'

Those go straight to the fireback.

There are, however, two invitations I would find irresistible. The first would start: 'Dear Mr. Parkinson, My committee would be delighted if you attended our dinner as guest speaker. My Rolls-Royce will meet you at the station and my wife (a former Miss Universe who, incidentally, is your biggest fan) insists you spend the night with us . . .'

The second would be to address an organisation like the Slough Karate Club (Ladies' Section) or the Great Britain Women Wrestlers Association. At present such invitations are conspicuous only by their absence in my mail.

The few invitations I have accepted have led to mildly disastrous evenings. The major problem is the system of allowing three officials of the club to precede the guest of honour in the speech making. It can be said without fear of contradiction that few of these gentlemen are good speakers and the problem facing the guest when he lurches to his feet, is not devising a means of keeping his audience awake, but finding a way of waking them up.

Having sat through more boring speeches than most, I am now able to predict with a fair amount of accuracy the length of every speech from the first sentence uttered.

'Unaccustomed as I am . . .' is not used much nowadays but when it is, it means that the speaker is so insensitive he is likely to go on for at least 30 minutes. 'I'm going to be brief . . .' is good for 20 minutes. The puzzling one is, 'I'm not much good at this job but have you heard the joke about the one-legged astronaut . . .?' The length of this speech depends on the reaction to the joke. If it's hearty then I can settle down for another half an hour; if it dies the death the speaker sits down immediately feeling disenchanted.

There are few variations on those opening themes. I did however come across one extraordinarily novel approach this year when a speaker stood up and said, 'I happen to have brought along my movie projector and screen and thought you might like to see a film of a trip I made . . .'

I frankly don't know a remedy to the boring speaker. To my knowledge the nearest anyone got to solving the problem was Fred Trueman, who on one famous occasion interrupted a speaker in full flow by tapping him on the arm and saying, 'Tha' wants to look sharp, t'beer's going sour in t'pumps.'

But in spite of all the horror that precedes him the guest speaker feels the real crunch when the time arrives for him to make a speech. Brain numbed from what has gone before, stomach soggy with roast turkey and Spanish claret, he is expected to scintillate.

People expect him to bubble with stories about what Fred said to Colin and what Brian said to Gary. They expect him to unravel the game's secrets, to clear up their nagging doubts, like is it true that E. W. Swanton's initials stand for Englebert Wobblychops; was Sir Alec Douglas Home really born in Barnsley; and is the D. C. S. Compton we see on telly the one that used to advertise for Brylcreem, or is it an impostor? And all he can do is contemplate the effect of cheap wine on a delicate stomach and wish he were a million miles away.

But there is no escape. One must soldier on and hope to God that they don't invite you next year, but even that is not guaranteed.

The best escape act of all was unwittingly invented by a friend of mine, who became so tired and drunk during the preceding speeches that when his turn came, he rose to his feet only to collapse face-first into a large and ripe Stilton cheese.

Later the club secretary suggested that a somewhat smaller fee than had been negotiated might be adequate because, as he tactfully put it, my friend 'had hardly given of his best.' Whereupon my friend, who was in no mood for being mucked about, said angrily:

'What do you mean not given of my best? If you don't like my act that's no fault of mine.' He got paid in full and was never invited back and considered himself doubly rewarded.

The only gentlemanly way out of the predicament is to be strong, to erect one's principles and then hide behind them. Which is why, in future, I shall say a polite but firm 'no' to all invitations . . . except those that carry hidden promise, like a meal with a roomful of lady wrestlers. I may sound disenchanted but the fact is I'm just a boy at heart.

22 The Wars of the Roses

There is no more certain indication of the decline of cricket
as a popular spectator sport than the pathetic attendance at
the present day Roses game. Once these were glorious en-
counters as important as test matches played to full houses
and the noise of battle on and off the field.

The fact of the matter is that today, except for a few nostal-
gics like myself, the prospect of a Roses game quickens as
many pulses in Leeds and Manchester as the news that the
Turkish Bank Rate has been increased to $6\frac{1}{2}\%$. Today the Wars
of the Roses is a tired headline to sell a story that people stopped
reading a long time ago.

It still meant something in 1947 when I went to my first
Roses game. We queued for three hours outside Bramall Lane,
Sheffield, and in that blessed moment when I was jostled
through the turnstile, I felt as if I had arrived in Paradise. We
sat on the hard concrete terracing of the football ground, knees
drawn up under our chins, arms pinioned by one's neighbours,
and there we remained for the next eight hours in a state of
acute physical discomfort sustained only by the knowledge
that this was no ordinary cricket match.

To stand up to relieve cramped muscles was to invite an
apple core or a pork pie crust to the back of the head along
with the usual polite advice to 'Sit thissen down Gladys.'

The Bramall Lane crowd has never been in sympathy with
the physical discomfort of others. A few seasons later I was

sitting on the same piece of concrete watching Yorkshire play Middlesex. It was during Compton's golden days when his face shone from every [hoarding] advertising hair dressing. In Yorkshire, among the rank and file cricket supporters, at least, there was always a guarded attitude toward Compton. He was too flash for their tastes, too much of a fly boy. Brylcreem and cricket don't mix in Yorkshire.

On this particular occasion Compton was granted a privileged insight into the way that the cricket lovers of Sheffield feel about the suffering of their fellow men. Yorkshire were batting when play was held up by the appearance on the field of what is called a Sheffield mongrel, which is to say a dog of exceedingly dubious parentage. The dog careered around the field defying the energetic attempts of the Middlesex side to catch it. It should be explained at this point that the sympathies of the Yorkshire crowd were entirely with the Middlesex men, it being a commonly held view in Yorkshire that dogs are for racing and not for petting.

Eventually it was Compton who caught it. It had to be, it was his year. He swooped low as the dog raced past him and scooped it triumphantly aloft. The crowd was relieved that the game could go on but remained unimpressed by Compton's panache. Still brandishing the dog Compton trotted towards the pavilion and as he did so the creature, being born in Sheffield and therefore no respecter of personalities, bit him smartly on the arm. Compton dropped the animal and stood rubbing the bite. The huge crowd watched the performance dispassionately and then someone from the football terraces shouted 'Put some bloody Brylcreem on it Compton.'

I digress only to acquaint you with my neighbours on that lovely Saturday in 1947 when I saw my first Roses game. There was a roar as Sellers, broad as a muck stack, won the toss and chose to bat. In the opening over I caught the sense of tradition and meaning that set these games apart and made them special. There was an atmosphere, a tenseness about the play which I have never tasted since, not even in a Test match. When Yorkshire lost their first wicket with only twelve scored the ground was in mourning. There came to the wicket an unknown called Smithson playing in his first Roses game.

In a situation calling for trench warfare Smithson decided on a cavalry charge. No one who sat in Bramall Lane that day could forget his innings. By any standards it was a good one, but in the context of the grim Roses games it was sensational. He defied tradition by hitting three fours and a three in one over, he made old men wince with his daring strokeplay and when he was out two short of his century every spectator creaked to his feet and applauded.

In his excellent book 'The Wars of the Roses' the late and very lamented A. A. Thomson recalls the innings and tells how, before Smithson went in to bat Emmott Robinson told him: 'Na, lad, what tha' has to do is shove thi' bat in t'blockhole and keep it there, chose 'ow.' When Smithson was out for 98 and with the cheers of the crowd still warming his ears, Emmott sought him out and reprimanded him for his 'outrageous levity.' At the end of the telling off Emmott was seen to shake his head despairingly and mutter, 'We'll never learn that lad.'

At the end of the day as we streamed out of grimy Bramall Lane, a cruffy, jostling, happy crowd, I felt privileged to have been initiated into cricket's most secret ritual. Warmed by the presence of 30,000 others I felt part of a tradition that would last for ever no matter what became of the rest of the game. In fact I was in at the beginning of the end. The tradition of the Roses game has not been enough to protect it from cricket's present maladies. What was once a meaningful occasion is nowadays just another three-day match.

Two years ago I went to Old Trafford for the Roses game. The morning sun shone, Old Trafford was beautiful, Trueman had his tail up, the Yorkshire fielding was of the highest and all these treasures were witnessed by a crowd so small it might have arrived in one double-decker bus. My mind drifted back to Sheffield in 1947 and I would willingly in that moment have swopped my seat in the stand for that concrete step if it meant a taste of the old excitement. I pitied any young boy being blooded that day at Old Trafford. His head full of dreams

and Cardus beforehand, he must have felt bitterly let down by what he saw.

In the bar I tried to start an argument but no one wanted to know. Completely disenchanted I found myself a lonely place in the sun and sat there sulking. Nothing altered my mood, not even the fact that at close of play Yorkshire were well on top. I went home knowing that things would never be the same again, that to recapture what used to be I must now rely on memory, Sir Neville and my old man. The consolation is that tradition dies harder with the players than the spectators and this fact at least will ensure that what happens in the middle during a Roses match will continue to be very different from the sort of thing that happens in any other kind of cricket match. The players of both counties are sufficiently well versed in their heritage to regard the Roses games as something special no matter how large the public apathy. I cherish one story told me by that fine Yorkshire cricketer Ken Taylor, now coaching abroad, that accounts for the reason why the Roses game will always be held to be different by the players. Taylor's first game against Lancashire was at Old Trafford. Yorkshire were doing badly as he walked down the pavilion steps on his way to the wicket. The Lancashire crowd was baying for blood. As he approached the pavilion gate it was opened for him by a uniformed attendant who, as Ken passed, politely saluted and then said out of the corner of his mouth: 'Best of luck lad, but think on, don't be long.'

Taylor was still bemused by this quote as he took guard. Unfortunately he was bowled first ball. He made his way sadly and slowly back to the pavilion. At the gate the same man was waiting. He opened the gate, touched his forelock and said: 'Thank you lad.'

23 Tale end

The cricket bag lay where I had thrown it one Sunday last August. It looked forlorn and unloved lying crumpled in the bottom of the wardrobe. Unpacking it was an awful experience to one as sensitive as myself. Every article gave out a musty reminder of that awful Sunday when I played my last game of the cricket season.

First, the boots, still sparkling white and newly spiked to remind me of my vanity. I had spent the night before the game giving them plenty of bull. As I worked I said to myself, 'Even though you can't play well you can always look lovely.' Then I came across my flannels with that grass-green patch on the backside, testimony to the catch I missed because I overbalanced and sat down as the ball curved towards me. It missed me by yards and dropped to earth quite gently while I sat there and watched it and the spectators bayed ruthlessly at my misfortune.

The only good thing to come out of that incident was a story offered in kind consolation by Malcolm Hilton. He was in my team that day, still spinning artfully and still not missing anything close in as in the great days at Old Trafford when Tattersall would bowl all day and Malcolm, Ken Grieves and Jack Ikin were in the leg trap catching everything. And still possessing that same unique, warm self-debunking humour delivered in plump Lancashire tones. That awful day as I sat there with the crowd jeering my misery he came up and said:

'Tha' knows one season I was in t'leg trap and were copping everything and we went to Blackpool and Washy (Cyril Washbrook) says to me as we come out of t'pavilion, "Does tha' reckon thissen at cover, Malcolm?" And I says "Tha' knows me skipper, I can cop 'em anywheer." So I goes to cover and this batsman gets reight under one from Tatt and up and up and bloody up she goes and I sets off after her.

'I'd been runnin' like a stag for two minutes and she's still going up and up and then she starts driftin' t'other way so I sets off back and soon I'm runnin' round in circles thinkin' "booger yer". And then she starts droppin' and I'm still tryin' to get under her and I'm shoutin' all t'time "She's mine, she's mine" to get t'others out of t'way. And then she drops and I dive for her and t'next thing I know I've knocked down t'wicket keeper, two men in t'leg trap and one set of t'stumps and t'bloody ball's ten feet away. And I'm laying theer wi' all this debris around me and I look up and theer's skipper lookin' down at me and he says "What other tricks does tha' know, Hilton?" So tha' sees anyone can drop 'em in this bloody silly game.'

But even that marvellous piece of Hiltonia didn't cheer me that terrible afternoon. And remembering it the other day as I cleaned my cricket bag was only small consolation.

Delving deeper into my bag I found my bat, the blade smooth and creamy like a young girl's skin. There was just one mark on it, a red scar high on the blade near the splice where I'd gone for a hook in the first over and had dollied a catch to the wicket keeper. As I looked at the evidence the horror of the moment came rushing back. The stroke was more than a piece of bad cricket, it was a breach of faith with my heritage. How many times had Maurice Leyland said 'Tha' does nothin' fancy for t'first fifty, tha' might start hookin' when tha's got a hundred, allus providin' tha's got thi' eye in, and tha' nivver late cuts until July.'

The words rang in my ears as I walked back to the pavilion, head bowed, conscience bloodied. I half expected to see Maurice on the steps waiting for me, brandishing his bat like a broadsword and saying 'Tha'll nivver learn sense will tha'.' Poor Maurice has gone now but I'll bet he's still playing pop with foolish youngsters wherever he may be.

I threw the bat into the corner of the room and swiftly emptied the remaining contents of the cricket bag on to the floor. At my feet lay the sum total of my achievements, the ruin of my ambition. Once, I thought, as I looked at the crumpled heap of my clothing and other people's cricket balls, once you could wear that lot and not do badly in any company. Once, I mused, wearing gear like that I played at Headingley, sat in Fred Trueman's seat at Bramall Lane, was bowled middle stump by George Pope, hit Illingworth for four (he wasn't trying), was cursed by Ticker Mitchell for dropping a catch and fielded first slip to Brian Close. But that was long ago. Now, I said to myself, you're like all that mob on the back pages, a failed sportsman turned sportswriter. A parasite living on memories.

It was then I decided never to play the game again. I thought about it coolly and decided it was the only thing to do. I resolved not to make any dramatic gestures like giving my gear away because in my experience the poor saps who have done that have been insincere. For instance I once played with a man who every time he had a bad patch gave all his gear away. The next week he would return and collect it from his friends and continue playing.

One day we decided to cure him of the habit and resolved that the next time he collected his gear we would only let him have it back if he paid us. It seemed to work quite well. The first occasion he tried to re-possess we told him it would cost twenty quid. He pleaded, cursed and was near to tears when we finally relented and settled for a large round of drinks from him in return. We congratulated ourselves when, after his next bad patch, he left the pavilion clutching his cricket bag without even a hint that he was thinking of quitting.

But our joy was short lived. The next week he appeared without his cricket bag and asked if he could borrow some kit. When we inquired what had happened to his equipment he said, 'Oh, I burnt that bloody lot last week.'

As I looked at the contents of my cricket bag I resolved not to do anything that foolish. I would make a quiet, unspectacular exit from the game. I would pack my bag, shove it in the wardrobe and there let it lie and moulder.

Pleased with the intelligent, unemotional way I had freed myself from a lifetime's addiction I set out for my monthly dozen down the street. I felt strangely elated knowing that there would be no more time wasted while I dallied with lost ambition, no more drinking from the bitter sweet cup of youthful memories. It was a flawless day and I could smell summer coming. What joy it will be in the coming months, I thought, to be free at the weekends to picnic or go sailing instead of being chained nervously to a pavilion seat.

In a field near my home youngsters were playing their first game of the season. I watched them for a while and pondered their coming disenchantment. One of them hit the ball towards me. I picked it up and held it for a moment. The lover parting from his lass, I thought. A boy came up and said 'Can I have the ball, sir?' 'With pleasure,' I said, and was about to hand it to him when I asked, 'Do you mind if I join in?' I don't know why I said it.

An hour later I was oiling my bat and dreaming of being Garfield Sobers. I can't help it if I'm cricket mad.

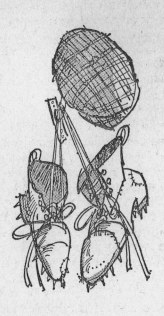

A selection of Arrow Books that will be of interest appears on the following pages:

THE ART OF COARSE GOLF   30p

MICHAEL GREEN

'One who, when playing alone, is regularly overtaken by women's foursomes.'

'One who normally goes from tee to green without touching the fairway.'

A lonely man, the Coarse Golfer. Separated not only from other golfers, but from the golf course as well. A trail of divots leading to a thicket. The sound of cursing and thrashing from afar. Somewhere out there the Coarse Golfer is at work . . .

'Michael Green's latest classic contribution to sporting literature.'   *Daily Mail*

'One of the funniest books about the game I have ever come across.'   *Birmingham Evening Mail*

MICHAEL GREEN

Moving house; or how to meet people but not make friends.

People like surveyors, who will point out the damp rot, the dry rot, and just general rot. People like the builders' men who will move in a lot of heavy tea-making equipment and settle down to a serious study of the racing pages. Or the electrician, who will announce that the house needs rewiring, take tea and attack the plastering.

A gas fitter will arrive with the wrong tools and go away forever. Two men will take the telephone away and leave a bill for reconnection charges. Assorted neighbours will complain. Finally a man from the Council will turn up to quote the fifteen Building Regulations that you have broken. You will have to start all over again.

MICHAEL GREEN

'Perhaps the only satisfactory definition of a Coarse Sportsman: One who when his club receives a grant from the National Playing Fields Association, wants to spent it on extending the bar.' The Coarse Sportsman comes in many shapes —most of them peculiar. He is enthusiastic— except when actually faced with a game. He is healthy— able to spend long hours on his feet in crowded bars. He is unlucky—Acts of God, blind referees or umpires, the Other Side and stray dogs always frustrate his most brilliant feats. He is sporting—always prepared to apologise to the man he has just crippled. Nor is he a coward—just abnormally sensitive to physical pain. He is the backbone of any game.

Michael Green is the author of the best-selling *Art of Coarse Rugby*.

The *Art of Coarse Sport* was originally published as the *Michael Green Book of Coarse Sport*.

THE ART OF COARSE RUGBY 20p

MICHAEL GREEN

'There aren't many sides these days who carry their posts to the park and change in an old garage. References to players biting each other have an unpleasant association now first-class players have started doing it . . .'

But 'somehow, somewhere, Coarse Rugby will flourish. Long may it continue to do so.'

From Michael Green's introduction to the paperback edition of his famous bestseller.

'The real stuff—quite the funniest I've read for years and much too good to be confined to rugger types.' *Richard Gordon*

Genuinely humerous—a weekend of laughs. *Yorkshire Evening News*

MICHAEL GREEN

You could say that *Even Coarser Rugby* takes over from where *The Art Of Coarse Rugby* left off.

Commencing with the Easter Tour, when hotel managers live in a state of siege and team captains kick their way out of locked wardrobes, Michael Green continues with a searching investigation of every aspect of the game, from sex in the selection committee to senility in the scrum, concluding with the Saga of Rodney and Fiona, that supremely nonsensical couple of with-it young things whose on-off romance has brightened many a Sunday afternoon for Michael Green readers.

A HISTORY OF BRITISH FOOTBALL 75p

PERCY M. YOUNG

The history of British football from the semi-legendary beginnings:

Violence: in 1303 an English footballer was killed by Irish students at Oxford. Earlier, it is said that the Anglo-Saxon inhabitants of Derby used not a ball but the head of one of their Danish enemies.

Professionalism: the first payment to footballers seems to have been made by the Prior of Bicester in 1425. The wage was 4p.

Rules: six-day games, everyone taking part, survival of the fittest.

From such starting points, Percy M. Young traces the entire development of the game—rules, referees, the first clubs, the formation of the F.A., the start of the Football League, professionalism—ending with the present day, the triumphs, and disasters, of international competition, the tactics of the modern game.

THE WORLD OF GOLD TODAY 45p

TIMOTHY GREEN

Gold: non-rusting, malleable, ductile, soluble in aqua regia (nitric and hydrochloric acid), molecular weight 197.0, specific density 19.3, melts at 1063° Centigrade . . .

Gold, in fact and fiction: the motive and occasion for theft, riot, murder, mayhem, romance and treachery.

Gold is mined, refined, cast, beaten and minted. It is hoarded, traded and smuggled. Gold is sensational news—'Bullion robbery'. Gold is solemn news—'World gold market crisis'.

The world of gold can be dramatic, complicated, mysterious. The workings of the world of gold affect us all.